190 restaurants wher

MILWAUKEE'S
BEST
Cheap Eats

Other books by Cari Taylor-Carlson

Milwaukee Walks: Twenty Choice Walks in a Classy City $7.95

The Upscale Outdoor Cookbook: Simple Recipes for Campers, Backpackers and Short-Order Cooks $8.00

Milwaukee Eats: An Insider's Guide to Saloons, Cafes, Diners, Dives and Neighborhood Restaurants (out of print)

The Food Lover's Guide to Milwaukee: An Insiders Guide to Ethnic Bakeries, Grocery Stores, Meat Markets, Specialty Food Shops and Cafes $12.95

Milwaukee Walks Again: 20 More Walks in a Classy City $9.95

To order add $3.50 for tax, postage and handling

Serendipity Ink
P. O. Box 511491
Milwaukee, WI 53203

190 restaurants where $15 still buys a meal

MILWAUKEE'S
BEST
Cheap Eats

Cari Taylor-Carlson
with Lynne Bergschultz

Serendipity Ink
Milwaukee, Wisconsin

Serendipity Ink
P. O. Box 511491
Milwaukee, WI 53203

First Printing 2000

Illustrations and Art Direction: Lynne Bergschultz
Graphic Production: Cheryl Gorton
Author Photograph: Don Gilmore
Editing: Gina Taucher
Printed by: McNaughton & Gunn, Inc.

ISBN   0-9629452-5-0

For Lynne Bergschultz,
illustrator, art director, fabulously creative artist, good friend,
procrastinator and personal cheerleader,

and Cheryl Gorton,
who patiently listens to me whine, then guides me through
the incomprehensible complexities of my Mac,

and Gina Taucher,
who tries to makes me sound like a writer.

CONTENTS

ACKNOWLEDGMENTS

Thanks to my friends and members of the Walking and Eating Society who reviewed restaurants for this book and cheerfully went where I sent them!!! Karen Brubakken, Kathy Locke, Doris Fons, Jo Cubbs, Pat Morris, Deb Servi, Peg Murphy, Mary Patek-Cheney and Ted Cheney, Lee Gierke, Nancie Baker, Tony Lo Bue, Chris O'Brien, Judy Laste, Betty White, Nancy Hamburger, Sue Smith, Wendy Janssen, and Bob and Sue Gibson.

INTRODUCTION

In 1993 I wrote *Milwaukee Eats*. Six years later, 60 of the original 118 restaurants are gone! This new book includes the 58 survivors plus 132 not included in that first book. Some of the 132 were unknown to me in 1993; most are newcomers. Does that tell us something about Milwaukee restaurants?

I won't belabor the obvious, except to suggest that a phone call might save you the inconvenience of finding "for rent" on the building instead of a welcoming smile at the door. It happens to me too, most recently at the former Mediterranean Breeze on Brady, now the site of Cempazuchi, a Mexican restaurant.

I'm excited about *Milwaukee's Best Cheap Eats*. *Milwaukee Eats* has been out of print for two years, and in demand ever since it sold out. It's fun to share my love of small restaurants with those who share my interest in diverse cuisines and the thrill of discovery. And, might I add, the thrill of the chase.

Suggestions from friends and other restaurant owners, local critics' commentary, and my insatiable curiosity led me to the 132 restaurants I visited over the past two years. Yes, it's taken that long to put this collection together!

I couldn't have completed this book without the Milwaukee Walking and Eating Society, for I was obligated to organize a group meal at a local restaurant every week for seven years. Furthermore, this is a group of people who enjoy unusual cuisine and diversity after their neighborhood walks. Everywhere we walk, I stick my nose in the door if a place looks like it might serve food. That's how I found the Hi Hat, McBob's, Tio Beta, and a few others.

It also helps to write about restaurants for *North Shore Lifestyle* Magazine and the *Outpost Exchange*. I enjoy meeting the people responsible for the food service, I love hearing their stories, and speaking as an entrepreneur, I know the value of good PR!

So here I am, promoting restaurants and hoping readers will follow my suggestions, be adventuresome, and find their way into some of these lesser known places in Milwaukee.

The restaurants in this book don't make fast food. If you want standardized, sanitized, homogenized food, go to Burger Chef and give this book to a friend!

When I started this two-year project, I had a plan. The cover blurb would promise, "If you don't get change from a $10 bill, it's not in the book." Despite the claim by Washington economists of a 1.6% rate of inflation for the last year, the cost of dining out has risen out of proportion to the rest of the economy. According to the *New York Times* (1998) the cost of a restaurant dinner has increased $1.43 each year since 1981. That suggests that in the six years since I wrote *Milwaukee Eats*, the cost of a $10 dinner has risen to approximately $18.58 and that's before adding 25% for tax and tip. Thus, the revised cover blurb reads "190 restaurants where $15 still buys a meal."

Here it is for your dining pleasure, *Milwaukee's Best Cheap Eats*, 190 restaurants where I promise you won't be bored and won't need a home equity loan to enjoy a nice dinner with tablecloths, flowers, candlelight and fine food. I've had a splendid adventure putting this together – now it's your turn!

Cari Taylor-Carlson

Abu's Jerusalem of the Gold

1978 North Farwell Avenue
277-0485
Lower East Side
Lunch, dinner every day - hours vary
Smoking-no
Bar - no
Bring cash
Dress: anything goes

– middle eastern –

Abu's is clean, cozy and no one will rush you through your meal. They don't open cans; everything is cooked fresh, and they guarantee authentic, real food.

The Baba Ghannouj is some of the best I've tasted in Milwaukee. It's a blend of roasted eggplant, tahini sauce, and spices served alongside warm pita bread. The hummos is a delicious mix of chickpeas, lemon juice, tahini, and again flavorful Mediterranean spices.

The eggplant pie, baked eggplant in a dough shell, tasted bitter but the tabbouleh was just about perfect. The salad contained so much parsley that it was colored parsley green instead of the usual bulgur or couscous tan.

The food goes down well with rosewater lemonade, and if your sweet tooth still needs a hit, finish with kanifi. It's bright orange, covered with something that looks like skinny angel hair pasta, and every bite oozes with honey sauce - highly recommended.

Acapulco

609 West National Avenue
647-8366
Walker's Point
Lunch, dinner every day
Smoking - yes
Beer and wine
MC, V, AE
Dress: casual, sombrero optional

– mexican

Warning: Don't start on the hot sauce until you have a cold drink in front of you!!! Acapulco serves one sauce - HOT - perhaps a disappointment to people don't have leather lips and sturdy stomachs, but if you like it hot, it's great washed down with a Mexican beer and a slice of lime.

Acapulco serves decent Mexican food with the usual tacos, tostadas, and a popular chicken fajitas plate. For less than $6 you can fill up on rice, beans and their famous chimichanga filled with chunks of beef. You won't find more food for less money in Walker's Point, and reviewers who don't usually opt for Mexican loved it.

African Harvest

4831 West North Avenue
445-2777
Milwaukee's West Side
Lunch and dinner Tuesday - Sunday
Smoking - yes
Bar - yes
Bring cash
Dress: bright colors

– african –

"I don't like spinach so don't bother to give me any." C.C.
Dukuly frequently hears this from visitors to her booth at
African World Festival. "Just taste it once and you'll like it," she
retorts with the confidence of a person who knows her food,
and is well aware that her Fried Stewed Spinach is a winner.
This is not a quickly thrown together dish, but one that takes
hours of preparation in the special mix of spinach, green
pepper, onion, celery and a few secret spices. C.C. brought the
recipe to Milwaukee from Liberia in 1981 when she fled her
country's civil war.

A house specialty is Jollof Rice, a blend of rice, African herbs
and spices, green peppers, tomatoes and onions, mixed
vegetables and tomato paste cooked and stirred until the color
and consistency reaches C.C.'s exacting standards.

During the week one can sample from a buffet at both lunch
and dinner. A typical spread will include long-grain rice, fried
rice with vegetables, two vegetable dishes and two meat dishes.
African Harvest is a friendly place, a place where one can eat
good food and, perhaps for the adventuresome, experiment
with new flavors and textures.

African Hut

1107 North Old World Third Street
765-1110
Downtown
Lunch and dinner Monday - Saturday
Smoking - no
Full bar
MC, V, AE
Dress: casual

– african –

Owners Yinka Adedokun and Moji Adedokun have created an African menu that challenges even those who are somewhat knowledgeable about their foods. Reviewers highly recommend the Peanut Stew, just like it sounds, served with rice, the Gondola Stew, tomato-based stewed vegetables with chicken, and the Beef Yassa, tenderloin chunks served in a wine sauce. Many of the entrees are served with a side of stewed spinach, or one can order the spinach as an entree and enjoy it aplenty with rice. The waitstaff will patiently explain the more unusual dishes, and may even offer a small sample to help one decide between Fufu and Egusi Stew, or Geelry's and Oran. The atmosphere is charming, with African objects d'art and cloth tablecloths.

Don't miss dessert!!! The African sweet potato pie, Odunkun, is plain yummy.

Aladdin

800 North Plankinton
271-9870
Downtown
Lunch Tuesday - Friday
Dinner Tuesday - Sunday
Smoking - only in specified area
Full bar
MC, V, AE
Dress: casual, no grubs

– middle eastern –

Aladdin is impressive. Not only does the waitstaff provide excellent and informed service, but the food is consistently delicious and if you're lucky, Chef Azmi Alaeddin will chat with you during your meal.

The menu is extensive, portions generous, and prices moderate considering the downtown location. Couscous with Chicken is especially tasty served in a sauce that's distinctly flavored but not overpowering. Dinners include lentil soup and warm pita bread.

Alaeddin came to America in the 1980s to go to school, and soon found himself cooking for student groups. In Kuwait where he grew up, he learned about the food business working in the family bakery. His experience served him well and gave him the courage to take the plunge and open a restaurant downtown with a promise to himself to offer only the finest customer service and cuisine.

The menu includes beef, lamb, chicken and seafood entrees and many vegetarian dishes. If you have room for dessert, try baklava, a rich yummy treat with phyllo dough, handmade by Chef Alaeddin.

Albanese's Tavern

701 East Keefe Avenue
964-7270
Riverwest
Dinner Monday - Saturday
Smoking - yes
Full bar
MC, V
Dress: celebrity casual

– italian –

S ix years ago they took out the pool table in the bar. Otherwise this is the same corner tavern where they've served homemade pasta for 39 years. The jukebox still cranks out golden oldies such as Frank Sinatra's soulful tunes, plus 60s memories from Lou Reed and Van Morrison.

Albanese's represents the best of the family-run Milwaukee restaurant / taverns. The menu, like the decor, hasn't changed much from 1941, and the younger generation continues the family tradition of reasonably priced, high quality Italian food cooked by Italians. There might be a short wait for a table on a weekend, but waiting in the bar area is easy and a great spot for people watching.

Many of us have been coming here regularly since the 1970s. Why this loyalty? You'll know when you try their antipasto with meats, cheeses, hot peppers and olives; homemade egg noodles smothered with spaghetti sauce; fresh garlic bread; spinach noodles in garlic sauce; outstanding pizza; and the not-to-be-missed chilled house red wine.

Three sisters, Fofe, Helen and Chris work the tables. The son of the original owner runs the business. This second-generation family hopes to pass on the recipes, the jukebox, the ambience and the house red to the next generation. Milwaukee hopes so too!!!

Al Calderone Club

2498 North Bartlett Avenue
964-5720
East Side
Lunch and dinner seven days a week
Open Saturday and Sunday at 2:00 p.m.
Non-smoke in the back room
Full bar
No credit, checks ok
Dress: business suits or tattered jeans

– italian –

Mention neighborhood Italian restaurants and Al Calderone Club will be one of the first on the list. What could give greater satisfaction than a reasonably priced Italian restaurant where one order of deep fried eggplant serves four? It's much too good to dip in marinara sauce – just drizzle fresh lemon juice over all and savor the taste of fresh eggplant done right. Those Italians excel at serving us irresistible fat calories. When the menu says "large pizza" they mean L A R G E - 15" x 19", a trayful of thin crust smothered with cheese, and if you order a house favorite, The Works, you get to sample everything except anchovies. Few leave without a doggie bag.

Eggplant parmigiano, mostaccioli, spaghetti, manicotti - all standard Italian food cooked by Italians. Mama Rosa presides over the kitchen, and the garlic bread hints of someone's passion for fresh garlic and lots of it. Don't ever tell Mama you don't like the food - "You tell them we have the best pizza in the whole world. Everything is made from old family recipes," explains Mama. Calderone's opens their back room for private parties and if you ask, they'll bake the birthday cake too. In summer an outdoor patio seats almost as many as the restaurant, and they play host to many rowdy summertime celebrations. Guess the word's out: good food, good prices and a few laughs in Calderone's backyard.

Al's Seafood Market

6922 West Good Hope Road
358-3014
Milwaukee's West Side
Open every day - hours vary
No smoking
No bar
Bring cash
Dress: comfy

– seafood - carryout only –

What if it's Friday and you've rented a movie? Come to Al's Seafood Market, where a steady stream of customers lined up on a frigid January night. Al sells buckets of seafood, seafood dinners, snacks, sandwiches, and seafood by the pound, all fried in low fat 100% cholesterol-free canola oil.

Al Hoell began his wholesale business selling seafood from a truck on Good Hope Road in the 1980s. At first he sold to restaurants, then being an astute businessman, he used his truck to sell retail during down time on weekends. Gradually Al's business expanded, and his formerly tiny shop has grown over the years to include a freezer seafood section, a small bakery, both fresh and smoked fish, soup du jour and a salad deli featuring a dozen delicious-looking salads.

Andrea's

5921 South Packard
483-2202
Cudahy
Open 24 hours a day, 7 days a week
Smoking - yes, non-smoking section
No bar
MC, V
Dress: respectfully, like a grandma

– anything goes –

Milwaukee has many family restaurants. This one's special. For example, four of the waitresses have been with Andrea's since the restaurant opened in 1990, regular customers are referred to as "family," and children who clean their plates are served free ice cream! Furthermore, on Thanksgiving, Andrea's serves a free meal to senior citizens. Last year they served 350 turkey dinners. Also for seniors, they offer a menu from 11:00 a.m. to 11:00 p.m. Monday - Thursday where no meal costs more than $5.95, and each dinner includes soup or salad, juice or cottage cheese, choice of potato, a bread basket, and dessert.

For the rest of us they offer three to eight $5.65 to $5.95 dinner specials every day. Stop in on Monday and choose from Baked Pork Chops, Hungarian Goulash or Roast Pork and Sauerkraut. This comfort food is available with or without 1950s Jell-O.

You can order breakfast all day and night with an enticing menu that includes crepes filled with sour cream topped with an orange-cointreau sauce, and raspberry crepes topped with real whipped cream. Not to be missed: the Belgium waffle with ice cream, strawberries, and whipped cream. Scrumptious!!!

Ann's Italian Restaurant

5969 South 108th Place
425-5040
Hales Corners
Dinner every day
Smoking - no
Wine and beer
MC, V, checks OK
Dress: some do, some don't - jeans fine

– italian –

Look for Ann's just off Highway 100 between a Chevy dealership and a NAPA Auto Parts store. The white clapboard bungalow doesn't hint at the well-established Italian restaurant inside. Nor does the interior. Don't expect a stereotypical Italian restaurant with red checked cloth tablecloths and multicolored candles in Chianti bottles dripping wax on your food. Instead, the owners decorated their three dining rooms in colonial / country style using teal and subtle reds, oak trim, brass wall sconces and arched windows. Vinyl tablecloths and bentwood chairs blend with the decor. Primitive prints of village and harbor scenes decorate the walls, along with a few needlepoint pictures that they'll sell in the lobby. Fiesta ware is displayed in a hutch.

Even the waitresses in khaki skirts and light blue tee shirts match the rooms, and they'll tell you about the house special, "pizza, the best you ever had." They know what diners come here to eat and they're absolutely correct. The thin crust pizza is delicious and prices reasonable. Reviewers comment, "I would pass up franchise pizza places closer to home to eat Ann's pizza." The entire menu with the exception of the Friday fish fry is available for carryout.

Antotonilco's

1100 South 11th Street
384-2678
Walker's Point
Lunch and dinner every day
Smoking - yes
Bar - yes
MC, V
Dress: serape optional

ATOTONILCO

- mexican -

Nothing's fancy here. The kitchen turns out steady, uninspired south of the border chow plus the usual rice, beans, and corn or flour tortillas. There are no surprises and no disappointments. You'll find a predictable Americanized Mexican menu with a whole fish prepared to your choice for $10 at the high end and Mole Con Pollo for $5 at the low end.

As soon as you're seated a waitress brings a basket of chips and a small bowl of red sauce. Warning: DO NOT dip into the sauce until safely fortified with a cold drink in front of you!!! They call this fiery sauce "mild" and if you ask, they'll bring a "hot" one.

Antotonilco's is a good choice for Mexican food if you're in a hurry, or in the mood for smaller portions. The flan was good and gone in six bites, and while yesterday's fried ice cream won't bring you back, the Alambres (spiced pork, green peppers, and onions in a tomato sauce) might.

Au Bon Appetit

1016 East Brady Street, Milwaukee
278-1233
Lower East Side
Dinner Tuesday - Saturday
No smoking in the restaurant
Full bar
MC, V
Dress: nicely

– middle eastern –

They haven't been here long, but they're here to stay. For the last three years Au Bon Appetit has been rated one of Milwaukee's 25 best restaurants. Co-owners Rihab Aris and Costi Helou created a soothing atmosphere far removed from the surrounding neighborhood. They spread cloth tablecloths on the tables, added fresh flowers and ruby red roses, placed art prints from Switzerland on the white walls, and hung lace curtains in the windows. They wrote, "Your Satisfaction is our Pleasure" on a brief customer evaluation, and one can sense that they take this motto seriously.

Each menu item is carefully displayed on the plate, and if presentation is rated A+, then their food deserves A++. You suspect when you open the door and sniff that something good is happening in the kitchen. It is! The Hummos Bethini has the right blend of garlic and lemon, the Baba Ghannouj has just a hint of sesame tahini and the rich flavor that comes from broiling the eggplant, and the falafel doesn't resemble anything that came from a box in the grocery store. Rihab Aris is an alchemist in the kitchen working with grains and beans and making magical flavors with garlic, olive oil, fresh lemon, parsley, and other classic Lebanese / Mediterranean ingredients. When we visited in February, Rihab was a work of art too, wearing a Valentine red chef's hat and her glowing smile.

Balistreri's

812 North 68th Street
475-1414
Wauwatosa
And . . . at their new location
5601 West Bluemound
258-9881
Lunch and dinner Monday - Friday
Dinner Saturday and Sunday
Smoking - no
Bar - yes
MC, V, AE
Dress: West Side chic

– italian –

They don't take reservations at Balistreri's (they will take them at the new Bluemound location) but the smiling waitresses make sure no one has to wait until they're cranky. Since there's not a formal bar, they serve beer and wine from the pizza carry out window. Come on a Saturday and the early dinner crowd includes young families and multi-generational groups. Food prices are reasonable and despite daily specials listed on a trendy chalkboard, most tables hosted pizza trays. Here is Milwaukee's West Side pizzeria.

Their French-fried veggies are popular. The zucchini served in a basket with lemon wedges and marinara sauce was surprisingly crisp inside a fried crust. The pizza's thin crust supported a melange of add-ons. Clearly this is knife and fork pizza at its best. At Balistreri's the management is sensitive to customer comfort and when the crowded restaurant heated up, instead of opening a door and letting the north wind blow, they turned on the air-conditioning just long enough to bring back the comfort zone. But then what would one expect from an Italian restaurant with Christmas lights in March and larger than life Snoopys dressed in Saint Patrick's Day green hanging from an old fashioned tin ceiling?

Balkanian New Star-Maric

901 Milwaukee Avenue
762-6397
South Milwaukee
Lunch and dinner every day
Smoking - yes
Bar - yes
Will take checks
Dress: for a walk - the restaurant is close to Grant Park

– middle eastern –

Everything's homemade here, including the bread and the feta cheese. They make a melt-in-your-mouth burek, and dinner is preceded by a plate of fresh tomatoes, bread and cheese. Don't miss the unusual cream of mushroom soup, and wash it down with a bottle of Yugoslavian beer. Owner Branko Maric will make you feel at home in his restaurant. Don't be in a hurry – this is a place for a leisurely dinner.

Barnacle Bud's

1955 South Hilbert Street
481-9974
Bayview
Lunch and dinner every day
Closed January and February
Smoking - yes
Bar - yes
MC, V
Dress: nautical navy blue and white deck shoes

– pub food –

There's no place else like Barnacle Bud's in Milwaukee, but first you have to find it. Take Becher east off Kinnickinnick, follow the signs to Skipper Bud's, and eventually you'll see signs for Barnacle Bud's and end up in a parking lot alongside the lovely Kinnickinnick River. The restaurant's décor is, of course, nautical. Outside, a deck overlooks the river and faces downtown, Continental Grain, and Medusa Cement. You'll have a front row seat for the evening light show as darkness slips past the skyline and windows light up in the buildings.

Pretend you're on vacation because that's what being on this deck feels like. It's a great place to sip a brew, while you admire the docked yachts nearby and sniff the air, full of the summer gassy odor of a northern marina. The Friday fish fry is popular. Try it and you'll know why.

Whether you arrive in one of those yachts or something more modest, as I did, finding a place to park can be a challenge on a summer evening. We left the boat downriver and climbed a fence. Not recommended.

Beans and Barley

1901 East North Avenue
278-7878
Lower East Side
Breakfast, lunch and dinner every day
Smoking - no
Wine and beer
MC, V
Dress: Lower East Side trendy

– gourmet vegetarian and much more –

Beans and Barley is the real thing. A genuine Lower East Side eatery with a menu that ranges from chicken entrees to vegan specialties and even a classy wine and coffee bar. In *Milwaukee Eats* in 1993 I wrote, "If a vote was taken for the most artsy food presentation, Beans and Barley would easily win...." Shortly after I reviewed it, the restaurant burned to the ground. In record time, the owners rebuilt, and fashionable eastsiders returned en masse to their healthful cafe, a place to sip a latte and enjoy a delectable meal.

On a blustery January morning it was a fine place for breakfast. Tall window walls look out through greenery onto North Avenue where traffic and people-watching can entertain a lone diner. Cornmeal Pancakes with Cranberry Compote make a delicious and filling breakfast, especially when accompanied by a banana smoothie. Insider information revealed the secret ingredient in the smoothie, nutmeg.

Beans and Barley is a feel-good place where healthy foods are served in an aesthetic manner by an artist-chef. They offer an extensive catering service, and a gorgeous deli with salads, entrees, muffins, scones, breads, La Boulangerie's morning buns, and yummy oversized cookies. For the daily specials, call 278-7800 for a recorded message. Now that's cool.

Bemo's

7413 West Greenfield
453-9094
West Allis
Dinner Monday - Saturday
Smoking - yes
Full bar
MC, V
Dress: leave your tie at home

– pub food–

This is another typical Milwaukee neighborhood restaurant / bar with good food. It's clean, well lit and not too noisy (as in, one can converse with a friend across the table), and has a great selection of imported beers and cider. Reviewers recommend Granny Smith cider

Watch for daily specials and expect to pay between $4.95 and $11.95 for a meal.

Benjamin Briggs Pub

2501 West Greenfield Avenue
383-2337
South Side
Lunch Monday - Friday
Dinner Tuesday - Saturday
Smoking - yes
Full bar
MC, V, AE
Dress: business attire at lunch, otherwise jeans/flannel shirts

– old milwaukee saloon pub food –

Benjamin Briggs originally housed a Schlitz tavern. In those days beer cost a nickel and came with a free lunch. The Schauer family bought the former beer hall in the 50s and ran a restaurant in the back room. Since 1990, the place has had a new owner and a new name, Benjamin Briggs Pub.

The Old World atmosphere is enhanced on the outside by ivy-covered brick walls and an old Schlitz sign. Inside, English pub decor suits the historical ambience. Wood floors, beamed ceilings, wood paneled walls, curio cabinets, German steins and Milwaukee artifacts set the stage for unhurried casual dining.

Benjamin Briggs Pub was named Milwaukee's best new restaurant in 1991 by *Milwaukee Magazine* and yes, they do find the good ones! The sandwiches are big. The half pound hamburger will satisfy most hearty appetites. The combo appetizer plate, potato skins, mozzarella marinara, and Buffalo wings, doubles for a meal. In fact, any of the appetizers will turn into a meal, especially with the addition of their delicious homemade soup or chili. The beer batter cod fish fry on Friday ranks with the best.

They're busy at lunchtime during the week and the decibel level does accelerate, but sometimes that's nice, because then a table of two will find themselves alone in a crowd.

Benjamin's Delicatessen and Restaurant

4156 North Oakland Avenue
332-7777
East Side
Breakfast, lunch and dinner 7 days a week - hours vary
Smoking - no
Wine, beer, a few mixed drinks
MC, V, checks ok
Dress: low key, a babushka perhaps?

– jewish kosher-style deli –

A steady flow of customers comes to Benjamin's from breakfast until closing, and owner Benji appears to be on a first-name basis with most of them. Everyone's comfortable here. Young couples drop by for a bowl of soup and a sandwich, and retired gents settle in for coffee, breakfast, international news, and local gossip. No one's in a hurry though - the service is excellent and somehow one friendly, efficient waitress manages all the tables.

It's a small place, with half the space used for the deli and the rest for the restaurant. Benjamin's has a dozen and a half tables, a small counter and the sort of orderly clutter that makes a house a home. An eclectic art collection on the walls adds to the cozy atmosphere.

Attention cinnamon bun lovers! Benjamin's serves a blue ribbon cinnamon roll that they have to slice because it's so fat. Forget calories. It drips with powdered sugar and butter frosting. The rest of the menu is typical Kosher-style deli food including a sandwich roster, soup, omelets, blintzes, and dinners starring brisket, boiled beef and roast tongue. They also serve herring, sardines, lox, gefilte fish, chopped liver and chicken soup with a choice of matzo ball, kreplach, noodles, kaske, or rice.

Black Tie Catering and Deli

2509 East Oklahoma Avenue
769-7945
Bayview
Monday - Saturday 8:00 a.m. to 8:00 p.m.
Smoking - no
Bar - no (but darn good coffee)
Bring cash, will take checks
Dress: in style, don't need to wear a tux

– gourmet deli food –

A gas station set in a triangle bounded by New York, Oklahoma and Delaware Avenues has had a new tenant for several years. In 1992 Black Tie Catering opened a delightful deli and café here. After establishing a reputation as one of Milwaukee's finest caterers, Michel and Jennifer Goetzinger brought their gourmet cuisine to their cafe.

Don't expect to come twice and find the same menu, as the specials change each week. Weekend catered events often precede weekly specials. Why not prepare extra veggie pate if you've already made enough for 300 over the weekend? This way the deli menu stays fresh and exciting and offers customers a chance to sample specialties created by two talented chefs.

As this book goes to press, rumors persist of a move by Black Tie, either to the site vacated by Wagner's almost next door, or to a larger facility on Clement Avenue. Stay posted.

Bodolino's

3124 North Downer Avenue
964-9616
UWM area, Lower East Side
Lunch and dinner every day
No smoking in the dining room
Full bar
MC, V, AE
Dress: like a student, wear a backpack

– pizza, etc. –

For some reason Bodolino's has a reputation for being a
veggie restaurant. Yes, they have a veggie chili, a veggie
platter with a dip, a veggie melt, a veggie burger and veggie
lasagna, but they also serve a traditional chili, a variety of
burgers, deli sandwiches with bacon, ham, turkey, and tuna, as
well as spaghetti and mostaciolli each with meat sauce.

The lasagna is outstanding, the mostacioli fair. The most
intriguing menu choice is the Gourmet Pizza, a thick crust
smothered with your choice of artichoke hearts, spinach,
tomato, broccoli or pesto, plus romano, mozzarella or feta
cheese. Now there's tasty veggie food.

If you don't have time to stop at the library, bring a book, leave
a book or take one and bring it back. Everyone does it, and one
is on the honor system.

Boobie's

502 West Garfield Avenue
263-3399
Near North Side
Lunch and dinner every day
Smoking - yes
Full bar
MC, V, AE
Dress: anything goes (headlamp and a
    magnifying glass to read the menu)

– bar food –

Boobie's may be the only restaurant in this book where we found a funeral hearse parked in front at 9:00 p.m. Post- or pre-funeral we wondered? Otherwise we found an upscale place with lively music that drowned the sound of the two TVs behind the bar, and a dark interior where a flashlight would come in handy when the time came to read the fine print on the menu. We ordered the Boobie's burgers based on their reputation, and shared onion rings and fries. The food was good, not outstanding, but in retrospect, one should order from the other side of the menu. Remember it was dark, and we neglected to turn our menus over. Had we checked both sides we would have found dinners with prices that met our budgets and a fine selection of steaks, chicken, pork chops, BBQ ribs, catfish and for lovers of soul food (and that includes this writer), collard greens, yams, and red beans and rice.

Boobie's is known for the live blues on weekend nights after 9:00 p.m.

Bosch

Corner 108th and Janesville Road
427-1400
Hales Corners
Dinner Monday - Friday
Lunch and dinner Saturday and Sunday
Smoking - only at the bar
MC, V, AE
Dress: blue jeans casual, bring earplugs on weekend nights

- pub food -

The building dates to the turn of the century, which explains its awkward location at the intersection of Mayfair and Janesville Roads. The interior is rustic and cozy with a fireplace for a blustery Milwaukee winter evening.

There's a rumor that the chef uses Cheez Whiz™ for the nachos, but the Cobb salad is delicious even if it didn't quite fit inside its serving dish. One can hardly go wrong with a bar burger, and Bosch's are no exception, or they'll sell you a turkey sandwich, a Rueben, brisket, chicken breast or a Mounded Sliced Beef Sandwich.

Be sure to tell your waitperson that you prefer the appetizer before the main course - they're likely to mix things up if they're busy, which they often are.

Boulder Junction Charcoal Grill

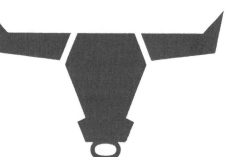

12550 West Burleigh Road
790-0726
Brookfield
Lunch and dinner every day
Smoking - yes in the bar
MC, V, AE
Dress: optional

– steaks, pub food and more –

Before you jump in the car and drive west to the 'burbs for dinner at Boulder Junction, be forewarned, the restaurant is noisy. The decor is fascinating though, with plenty of western art, stuffed animals, farm implements and harnesses to look at while you wait for a table. The wait will be short, thanks to an efficient staff and the large number of patrons who come to drink and to share just an appetizer before moving on. Thus, a crowded bar doesn't necessarily mean a long wait for dinner.

All the meat they serve is grilled over charcoal, and in addition to a burger menu, they'll grill you a steak including fillet, ribeye, porterhouse or top butt. The steaks come in many sizes, from a ladylike 6-ounce fillet to the "Grand Canyon of steak! Guaranteed to fill your boots," a 24-ounce porterhouse for $24.95.

If you yearn for a 1950s dinner, order pan-fried calves liver, or if you prefer the 90s, order vegetarian stir-fry. In other words, there's something for every taste.

Brady Street Pharmacy

1696 North Astor Street (corner Brady and Astor)
272-4384
Lower East Side
Breakfast, lunch and dinner every day
Smoking - yes
Bar - no
MC, V, will take checks
Dress: Doc Martens and leather

– 1950s drugstore chow –

E very Sunday at noon, it's almost impossible to find an open table at this neighborhood hangout. Several groups have been spotted dining, drinking unlimited cups of coffee, and solving the problems of the world at the same time every day. They appear to stay for hours. It might be the food that brings them, for some of the 1950s meals are quite tasty. I don't recommend the open face hot turkey sandwich, but it is a strong reminder of childhood, and pre-cholesterol memories of spooning the last drops of gravy over Wonder Bread.

I do recommend the chicken salad sandwich and the club sandwich. Chicken salad came on toasted whole wheat bread and contained lots of tender chicken and minimal mayo. Likewise the club came filled with a generous portion of turkey.

You won't find my favorite breakfast on the menu. Ask the waitperson to prepare a Belgium waffle, add two scoops of ice cream, preferably butter pecan, and pour a half-cup of warm syrup over all.

Brewed Awakenings

1208 East Brady Street
276-2739
Lower East Side
Breakfast, lunch and dinner every day
Smoking - yes (also a non-smoking room)
Bar - no
Bring cash
Dress: dreadlocks for guys and early Goodwill

- great cafe chow-

This San Francisco coffeehouse clone serves delicious food along with their caffeine drinks. In addition to the usual coffeehouse menu, you'll find soy milk for people who are lactose intolerant, and textured vegetable protein added to the veggie chili. Baking is done in-house and their focaccia is one of the best I've tasted in Milwaukee. Instead of olive oil and tomatoes on thick Italian bread, this focaccia is a thin cousin with olives, rosemary, oregano and basil baked on top. The crisp crust retains the flavors without covering them with oil.

Carrot-rice soup is yummy, lightly seasoned with basil, garlic, oregano and a hint of turmeric for color, and the dark cherry muffin tasted like a muffin should, with a dense tunneled interior and enough cherries to justify calling it a cherry muffin.

At last Milwaukeeans have joined trendy New Yorkers or Californians with their passion for coffeehouses, especially one like Brewed Awakenings, where the food matches the fine coffee and lingering over a latte and the *New York Times* is a respectable pastime.

Broadway Bar and Grill

223 North Broadway
272-8440
Historic Third Ward
Breakfast, lunch and dinner Monday - Saturday
Smoking in the coffee shop only
MC, V dinner only; breakfast and lunch bring cash
Dress: depends on when you come - jeans during the day,
   chic at night

– coffee shop grill daytime...
upscale cuisine at night –

C an a restaurant have two personalities? Broadway Bar and
Grill is trying to be both coffee shop and upscale
restaurant. Certainly the Third Ward needs more restaurants to
feed the suit-and-tie crowd who arrive after 6:00 p.m. for pre-
theater dinner or post-theater drinks and snacks.

By day, this restaurant is a local hangout for people who work
in the area, many of whom have been coming here for years. It
was popular long before the Third Ward became gentrified,
bringing customers from the 'burbs to this former warehouse
district south of I-794. The Broadway has always been a place
where one can get a real burger, juicy, greasy, but guaranteed to
be good to the last drop that runs down your chin. A $3 the 1/3
pound cheeseburger served with fries is a generous meal.

In November 1997, the Grill changed hands and opened for
dinner. The price goes up for the dinnertime burgers, but so
does the size from 1/3 to 1/2 pound, and at night it's known as a
"Broadway Burger." They also offer pasta dishes, shrimp,
chicken, and for the Friday fish fry, Sicilian-breaded cod or
perch. The wine list is impressive, for the owners are wine
connoisseurs. Wish them well in this chancy restaurant
changeover.

The Brown Bottle

221 West Galena - inside the Schlitz Park Office Complex
271-4444
Lower East Side just west of the river
Lunch and dinner Monday - Friday
Dinner only on Saturday
Closed Sunday
Smoking - yes
Full bar
MC, V, AE
Dress: fashionable

– bar food –

A brief history lesson first. The Schlitz Brown Bottle opened in 1938 to commemorate the introduction of the brown beer bottle as a repellent against the negative effect of sunlight on beer. For the taproom, management hired artisans and craftspersons to recreate a typical European inn of the 1800s. Many years of research were devoted to this project, including numerous trips to England to collect objects of art to add to the Old World charm of the Brown Bottle.

No detail was overlooked and today the owners are very proud, and rightly so, of this impressive recreation of 19th century grandeur. Reviewers found the food good but not exceptional. Their waitress suggested an order of chicken tenders along with an entree, but since they thought this was too much food, they saved the tenders for après dinner. As it turned out, the tenders, deep-fried and served with BBQ sauce were the culinary stars of the meal.

Bunker's Mainstreet

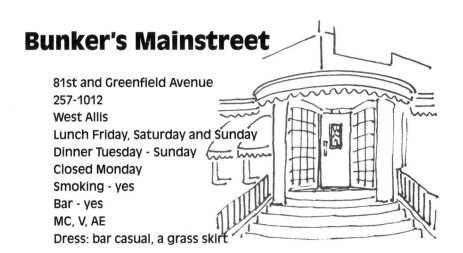

81st and Greenfield Avenue
257-1012
West Allis
Lunch Friday, Saturday and Sunday
Dinner Tuesday - Sunday
Closed Monday
Smoking - yes
Bar - yes
MC, V, AE
Dress: bar casual, a grass skirt

– caribbean and regular pub food–

It's a casual, friendly place and a sampling of their excellent tavern food shows what separates Bunker's from an ordinary Milwaukee bar. Since it's a tavern, don't be surprised when they crank up the rock music. The smoke index rises along with the decibels. The place is visually stimulating as well, with many televisions, all turned on; beer signs, serapes, mirrors and fish tanks decorate the walls.

Bunker's has a creative selection of bar burgers including Bayou Melt, a Cajun burger on rye, and Dudley Do Right, a burger smothered in jack cheese with Canadian bacon. For vegetarians and pizza lovers, they make a white pizza, no red sauce, and a garden pizza with more than a hint of garlic.

Cafe at the Plaza

1007 North Cass
272-2494
Lower East Side
Breakfast and lunch Monday - Saturday
Breakfast only Sunday
Smoking - only in the hallway,
    not in the restaurant
Bar - no
Bring cash
Dress: Lower East Side chic

– cafe style food –

Sheila's Cafe at the Plaza is a tough act to follow, but the current owners are doing a great job of continuing to serve good food. The muffins are delicious, and so are the omelets. If you're hungry, order the veggie three-egg omelet with hash brown potatoes and prepare for a meal that lasts through breakfast and lunch. Also recommended, the croissant sandwich served with potatoes. Don't be put off by American cheese in the sandwich, it's still good and filling.

The waitstaff is cheerful and efficient, and when thirty Walking and Eating Society members came to breakfast and everyone ordered an omelet, the chef didn't miss a beat as she gracefully served thirty veggie omelets with potatoes and rye toast spread with real butter. While they waited, all enjoyed plentiful, strong Alterra coffee.

Cafe Knickerbocker

1030 East Juneau Avenue
272-0011
Downtown
Breakfast, lunch and
    dinner every day
Smoking - no
Bar - yes
MC, V, AE
Dress: downtown chic

– fancy food –

As I write, the Knickerbocker is closed for several months for major remodeling, but you can be sure that when they reopen the food will remain their strong suit, and only the space will be different. In the old Knick, the first thing you saw when you walked into the restaurant was the desserts. Try "September 7th" if you have a chocolate craving, for this creation starts with vanilla mousse, and moves into serious chocolate with a wrap of chocolate mousse and bittersweet chocolate buttercream frosting. The inspiration for this torte came on September 7th, hence the name.

The menu at the Knick is consciously designed for those who appreciate fresh, simply prepared foods. They offer three wholesome meals a day and hope to draw some of the same diners for more than an occasional breakfast, lunch, or dinner. The chef prepares wonderful salads. Of note is the Caesar salad, served with a choice of chicken, tuna or smoked salmon. A delicious light lunch or dinner that could be beefed up with the addition of soup du jour or a September 7th dessert.

The Knick's deck is one of the best in the city with a view of Lake Michigan and a fresh breeze on a steamy summer day. I look forward to the remodeled, "new" Knickerbocker.

Cafe Vecchio Mondo

1137 Old World Third Street
273-5700
Downtown
Lunch and dinner Monday - Saturday
Smoking - no
Full bar
MC, V
Dress: with class

– simply prepared gourmet –

On a chilly Saturday morning in November, twenty members and guests of the Milwaukee Walking and Eating Society enjoyed an early lunch at Cafe Vecchio Mondo. A set menu included a turkey sandwich with green peppers, artichoke hearts, mozzarella cheese, and pepperoncini on focaccia bread; pasta salad; and coffee. This seemingly ordinary lunch turned into a superb meal as the hot sandwiches came off the grill. The response was unanimous. Twenty people bit into their sandwiches, looked around and in unison said, "Ohhhhhh this is really good."

Why were the sandwiches so special? Perhaps it was the focaccia bread or the fresh ingredients, or could it be the grill that just arrived from Seattle? The grill is a "panini" maker, an oversized waffle iron that works without oil or butter. Pressure toasts the outside and melts the cheese without detracting from the integrity of the rest of the ingredients. Don't miss the Vegetarian, with layers of grilled eggplant, green pepper, portabella mushrooms, cheese, red onion, artichoke hearts, lettuce, and fresh basil. Everything at this cafe is superb and owner-chef Russ Davis is on hand to supervise the kitchen. This restaurant is truly a class act!!!

Carini's La Conca d'Ora

3468 North Oakland Avenue
963-9623
Shorewood
Lunch and dinner Tuesday - Friday
Dinner Saturday and Sunday
Closed Monday
Smoking - yes (non-smoking room)
Bar - yes
MC, V
Dress: nicely

– italian –

It's hard to find the entrance to Carini's on Oakland, but if you look carefully you'll see it next to Siegel's Liquor Store. Owner Peter Carini came to Milwaukee in 1966 from Porticello, a small fishing village near Palermo. When he was growing up, he watched his mother cook, and found magic in her ability to turn ordinary ingredients such as tomato puree and tomato paste into a delicious light sauce. "A good Italian sauce is made by taste and touch, instinct perhaps, but not from a recipe," his mother told him. Peter is still trying to duplicate his mother's tomato sauce, but thinks he might be getting close.

With twenty years of professional cooking under his belt, Peter Carini knows what he's doing in his spotless kitchen. He cooks fresh foods in a simple manner and doesn't spare olive oil, fresh basil or garlic. The dinner entrees tend to be over the top pricewise for this book, but his lunch buffet for $5.95 is not to be missed. La Conca d'Ora means "shell of gold" and refers to the beauty of the mountains, the Mediterranean Sea and the "glow" that occurs morning and evening in Porticello.

Casablanca

730 West Mitchell Street
383-2363
South Side
Lunch and dinner
   Tuesday - Sunday
Closed Monday
Smoking - no
Bar - yes
MC, V
Dress: a veil perhaps, certainly casual prevails

– middle eastern –

Since I wrote *Milwaukee Eats* in 1993, Casablanca moved from a Mitchell Street location to Oakland Avenue and back again. Now, back where they started, one of the best deals around is the Tuesday - Friday All-U-Can Eat Vegetarian Lunch Buffet for $4.95. This includes a drink and a mouthwatering selection of entrees from the menu, such as vegetarian stuffed grape leaves, hummos, babaghannoj, spinach pie, tabouleh, falafil, and vegetarian couscous. Even if you can't pronounce some of these foods, come to taste, and you won't go away hungry or disappointed.

Otherwise, browse the menu and choose from a delectable listing of salads, sandwiches, and beef, lamb, or chicken entrees. Casablanca also offers a mouth-watering selection of appetizers besides the ones on the buffet. The Foule, fava beans cooked in olive oil and spices served with warm pita is delicious, as is the stuffed grape leaf appetizer, both vegetarian and non. You can order shawarma for a dinner entrée or shawarma in pita bread with tahini sauce and onions for lunch.

Cataldo's

815 East Brady Street
276-6004
Lower East Side
Dinner every day
  (very late night menu for night owls)
Smoking - yes
Full bar
MC, V
Dress: leather and chains after 2:00 a.m.

– italian –

H ere's a place I've driven past dozens of times without stopping, until another restaurant owner told me about their fantastic food. He's right!!! Located at the west end of Brady Street, Cataldo's red and green exterior fits perfectly into this Italian section of town. The neighbors know the food's great and they're frequently present. It's not what one would call chic, but owner Carlos serves Sicilian food from his native Italy and Cataldo's is as good a pizza and spaghetti place as any neighborhood restaurant in Milwaukee.

The pizza ingredients sit on top of a homemade crust; the pizza is always made with fresh veggies and plenty of red sauce and cheeses. The pasta entrees are served with the house tomato sauce, but if you want to spend another $1, the cook will add their special chunky tomato marinara sauce.

Don't miss the lasagne, a generous portion, and a Walking and Eating Society favorite dinner at a favorite restaurant on fashionable Brady Street.

Cempazuchi

1205 East Brady Street
291-5233
Lunch and dinner Tuesday - Saturday
   Dinner only on Sunday
Smoking - only in the bar
Credit-V MC AmEx
Dress-something colorful

– mexican, specialities from oaxaca –

In April, 1999 an exciting restaurant opened on Brady Street. If fine dining and Mexican cuisine sounds like they're mutually exclusive, then a visit to Cempazuchi at the corner of Brady and Franklin Streets, across from the fire station, will surely reverse that commonly held perception. The colors of Mexico, burnt orange, sky blue, hot pink and soft gold dominate, while one's attention is drawn to Day of the Dead artwork on one wall, hand woven serapes, ceramic planters and other artifacts on the windowsills.

For the past 10 years, co-owners Bryce Clark and Sal Sanchez have traveled often in Mexico and along the way developed an appreciation of fine dining Mexican style. Classic Mexican cuisine, and that does not include Tex-Mex tacos, burritos, enchiladas and tostadas, is one of complicated preparation and is considered in gastronomic circles on a par with fine French cooking. As in French cuisine, some of the best and most complicated sauces star in dishes such as Tamale Oaxaqueno, $12.95 or Guelagetza $13.95. These dishes share a common sauce, Oaxaca's famous negro mole, a rich dense sauce that Chef Sanchez uses on a base with a mild flavor since the star is the sauce and what's underneath, the palette.

Dessert lovers won't want to miss Natillas, an egg-based custard cooked on top of the stove. Don't plan to share, it's too good! Buen Apetito!

Centennial Bar and Grille

10352 North Port Washington Road
241-4353
Mequon
Lunch and dinner every day
Smoking - yes
Bar - yes
MC, V
Dress: North Shore yuppie, come in your sport utility vehicle

– good pub food –

"Come on a Tuesday night," owner Brian Roelle suggested. "We're not usually busy early in the week." As it turned out, "not busy" meant immediate seating but still, every table was taken. The restaurant, originally built as a home for Mathew and Lena Sherer in 1895 has been a tavern, a brothel, a community center, a repository for demon rum during Prohibition, and a showroom for antique cars. Why does being located in an old brothel house add spice to a restaurant? As they explain on the menu, "the patrons' appetites extended beyond food to the upstairs rooms."

Despite the crowds, one can count on good food served in a prompt manner and comfortable ambience, meaning you'll be able to carry on a conversation at the table. Sandwiches star here, with the Chicken Parmesan being one of the best. The grilled chicken breast is topped with sautéed mushrooms, marinara sauce and melted mozzarella cheese. Served with a side of coleslaw it's a meal in a bun. The Mequon Melt, ham, turkey, bacon, tomato, onion and cheese topped with Russian dressing is a winner, and so is the Cajun Burger with waffle fries. Save room for a slice of Keylime Cheesecake and leave with a full belly and a smile.

The Charcoal Pit

2641 North 27th
372-1090
Central City
Lunch Monday - Saturday
Smoking - definitely
Bar - no
Bring cash
Dress: truck stop casual

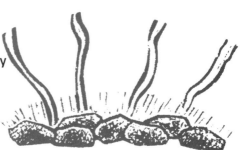

– burgers –

This was an interesting lunchtime burger. The "charcoal" could refer either to the color of the building or to the continuously glowing charcoal coals inside. And pit? I'll let the reader decide. The restaurant was easy to spot on the west side of busy North 27th Street, for there were three trucks idling in front, filling the available parking in the 2600 block. This place is straight out of a movie set from the 50s. Counter dining only on stools, some with backs and most without; all in a state of disrepair. People-watching is an art here; they come and go with carryout orders, but try not to stare. So is eavesdropping when we're all cozy together at the counter. The phone rings constantly and both slightly funky female employees can flip burgers, slap mayo on Kaiser rolls and talk on the phone at the same time.

To find meat underneath the pickle and onion, order a double. Paper laid on the counter serves as your plate, drinks include chocolate milk, and the menu is easy to remember - burgers, cheese or no; steak sandwiches ($1 each); and brats. To tell the truth, my burger was good, a double cheeseburger on a crusty roll for $1.85, but don't look at the ceiling or the floor, you might lose your appetite. I wouldn't go here alone again; I'd bring a friend!

The City Market

2205 East Capitol Drive
962-0100
Shorewood
Breakfast, lunch, and dinner every day
Smoking - no
Bar - no
MC, V, AE
Dress: stylish

– outstanding cafe food –

Word of mouth lures me to the most interesting places. Friends told me over and over again, "Cari you'll love City Market". They were right. Too bad the Market wasn't there when my car seemed to spend more time in the shop than out, and I needed a place to hang out and wait for the inevitable bad news. A cup of dark Market Blend Coffee and a cranberry nut scone might have improved my disposition.

This is a bakery, a café, and a restaurant where everything tastes good, from the coffee to the bread to the desserts, sandwiches, soups, salads and more. Full breakfasts include a quiche of the day and Market Strada. Each is served with fresh fruit and a muffin or a scone, more than enough for a single meal.

The bread is baked right behind the front counter, and sandwiches use these in-house breads. For example, Vegetable Stack comes on nine-grain bread and combines a healthful mix of veggies and cheeses.

Who could ask for more? Delicious food served in a charming space, small and intimate with wooden tables, soft green and rose colored walls and a carpet to contain the noise.

Conejito's Place

539 West Virginia
278-9101
Walkers Point
Lunch and dinner seven days a week
Smoking - yes
   (small non-smoking section)
Full bar
MC, V, AE
Dress: something washable

– mexican –

Conejito's used to be a small corner tap, but four years ago they knocked down some plaster and opened a spacious dining room adjacent to the original space. It's pleasant. They hung serapes on the wall for a Mexican touch, added a big bar, and now cater to younger crowds who prefer Sting to mariachi.

The new dining room solved the real problem at Conejito's - space. They had too many customers and not enough seats, but they still pack crowds into the original restaurant, where they squeeze the greatest number of bodies into the least space at community tables. To tell the truth, the food tastes the same in both places, but it's more fun to sit elbow to elbow and to meet someone while reaching across them for salsa. Lots of people come solo, and it's a comfortable place to do that.

Everyone's there for the same reason: cheap, consistently good Mexican food. Tostadas and Conejito's are synonymous in Milwaukee. They also offer plates of tacos and enchiladas and don't blink if someone orders one of each. They don't wash dishes here because they use paper plates, and instead of linen napkins, they pile paper ones on the counters and tables. A burrito requires three napkins and most mixed plates, especially the ones with tostadas, are four-napkin meals.

County Clare

1234 North Astor Street
272-5273
Lower East Side
Lunch and dinner every day
Smoking - yes
Full bar
MC, V, AE
Dress: a kilt and a cap

– irish etc. –

Even the salads are especially tasty at County Clare. Grilled Vegetables with Gorgonzola Cheese has nary a hint of nutrient-free iceberg but instead a colorful, flavorful montage of assorted greens presented with a vinaigrette dressing. Beyond lettuce, the salad includes two kinds of squash, red and yellow peppers, matchstick carrots and red onion, all served warm in a dinner-plate-sized bowl decorated with paprika and finely chopped parsley.

Likewise Smoked Irish Salmon Salad with Goat Cheese, made with salmon imported weekly from County Clare in Ireland was a treat. So was the Irish Root Soup, decorated with a floating sour cream shamrock sprinkled with chopped parsley. It tastes of the earth as it should, filled with sweet potato, leek and carrot.

The Grilled Chicken Sandwich with Caramelized Onion is delicious and so are the Corned Beef and Cabbage and the Corned Beef Hash. All fall under the $10 limit and for the price, you will be glad you visited County Clare; you may want to plan your return soon to explore some of the more pricey entrees.

Crawdaddy's

6414 West Greenfield Avenue
778-2228
Lunch Tuesday - Friday
Dinner Tuesday - Saturday
Smoking - yes in a separate dining area
Full bar
MC, V, AE
Dress: like a southern belle

– cajun –

Open just two years, Crawdaddy's is a star, featuring an extensive evening menu and an array of nightly specials. This Cajun restaurant slipped into the book, not because their prices met the "change from a $10 bill" criteria, but because the food is superb and a place that charges up to $19.95 for an entree and doesn't accept reservations must be hot. Reviewers raved about Blackened Walleye Cheeks on Wild Wilted Greens, Bourbon Chicken with Sweet Potatoes, Green Chili Marinated Washington State Sturgeon, and Macadamia Nut Crusted Hawaiian Tuna.

The budget conscious diner could order a classic New Orleans French Quarter Muffuletta ($5.95) or call one of the $6.95 salads a meal and choose from Marinated Grilled Lamb Salad, Grilled Chicken Salad, or Crawdaddy's Caesar Salad.

The waitstaff is friendly, efficient and impressively knowledgeable about the menu selections. Sometimes the dining room gets a little noisy, and the zydeco and blues music drown table talk, but that's part of the fun when one dines at a "hot" restaurant.

Dale's

6132 West Capitol
463-6920
Milwaukee's near West Side
Lunch Monday - Saturday
Dinner Monday - Friday
Smoking - yes
Full bar
Bring cash
Dress: surprise Dale with a clown suit

– soups and bar food –

The question is - how could I live in Milwaukee for twenty-seven years and just learn about Dale's? Granted, the square red brick building on a northeast corner of Capitol Drive doesn't look like a restaurant, and the sign looks like it's just another Milwaukee neighborhood bar. Don't be fooled. Trust me, Dale's is unique. Yes, it's a typical bar, but one can't help feel right at home when Dale himself takes your order, and if you ask, will tell you about the soup du jour. He makes a new soup every weekday without serving a repeat for six months!!! Each soup pot holds enough for two days, thus each day, one must make a choice. We sampled Stuffed Pepper Soup and Hungarian Goulash, thick with meat and vegetables and delicious. Dale wrote a cookbook, *104 Soups from Dale's*. It's for sale at the restaurant.

Try the Ostrich Burger, low fat, low cal, and low cholesterol, but you'd never guess it's healthy for it's juicy, especially when smothered with fried onions and cheese. Dale also offers a regular burger, seventeen grilled sandwiches, a deli menu, BBQ beef, chicken, or pork and a depression era Fried Egg Sandwich for $2.75.

In his spare time, Dale is a clown. He's a good man with a big heart and a wide smile!!

Dancing Ganesha

1692 North Van Buren
220-0202
West end of Brady Street
Dinner Tuesday - Saturday
Smoking - a non-smoking area
Full bar
MC, V, AE
Dress: fashionable yet exotic, wearable art

- indian -

Once in a while a restaurant bursts onto the scene with such force it's an overnight success, and at Dancing Ganesha we have a perfect example of this phenomenon. Instead of what is locally considered traditional Indian cuisine, chef / owner Usha Bedi has developed a lighter touch, a fusion menu. For example, you'll find ground turkey instead of beef in the popular samosa (a meat filled dumpling), and a variety of dishes that are deep-fried in healthful canola oil, plus a daily daal (lentils slow cooked with spices) served over basmati rice.

The name Dancing Ganesha comes from Ganesh, the Hindu god of prosperity and wisdom. He got his famous elephant's head thanks to his father Shiva's temper when he came home from a long trip and found his wife, Ganesh's mother, in bed with a young man. Unfortunately for Ganesh, he was the young man, and he lost his head to the sword. Pavati, his mother, forced Shiva to bring Ganesh back to life but this could only happen if Ganesh was given the head of the first living thing Shiva saw, which happened to be an elephant. It's a nice image, the God of Prosperity and Wisdom blessing this popular Indian restaurant.

De Marini's

1211 East Conway
481-2348
Bayview
Dinner every day
Smoking - yes
Full bar
MC, V
Dress: tuck your napkin at your neck or wear something
washable

– italian –

They have a great location in Bayview, and with a shortage of restaurants in the area, DeMarini's is a good dinner choice. They specialize in pizza and pasta, and they don't try to do more than the things they do well. Prices are reasonable; a 16" x 12" pizza with cheese, pepperoni, onions, and mushrooms costs $13.50 and generously feeds three. The chef doesn't scrimp on the toppings. Add garlic bread with marinara sauce for dipping, and a meal fit for a pizza lover is on the way.

Dino's Italian Restaurant

4252 South Howell Avenue
744-0990
South Side
Dinner every day
Smoking - yes
Full bar
MC, V
Dress: jeans

- italian -

All the portions are generous, everything's fresh, and Dino's salad can serve two hungry customers. Look no further for an outstanding pizza on the South Side - Dino's has it. Their claim to fame is thin crust pizza, piled high with cheese and your choice of add-ons. The house favorite, Dino's Special Pizza, a combination of sausage, mushrooms, onions and mozzarella brings a steady stream of regulars. Wooden booths around the perimeter of the dimly lit dining room provide privacy for enjoying an intimate evening of Italian cuisine.

Dino's Lounge and Restaurant

808 East Chambers Street
263-6033
Riverwest
Dinners Friday and Saturday
Fish Fry on Friday
Smoking - yes
Full bar
No credit cards, will take checks
Dress: like the locals

- italian -

Several years ago, someone told me about a place in Riverwest where Pepper Shrimp would bring me to my knees in exultation. It took months to track down this euphoric platter of fresh shrimp. Prepared in white wine sauce with delightfully crunchy red and green peppers, onion, tomato, and fresh mushrooms, Pepper Shrimp is served over homemade linguini with plenty of Italian bread to sop up the sauce. A salad accompanies dinner, and its homemade vinaigrette also deserves a slice of bread to avoid leaving a drop of extra virgin olive oil on the plate. We washed our meal down with Lakefront Brewery's Riverwest Stein Lager beer, and finished with cannoli from Sciortino's Bakery - a perfect ending.

Everything is made from scratch here by Chef Rita, and even the bread crumbs are seasoned by this talented cook; that hint of breading makes the Pepper Steak over Linguini especially delicious.

This family-run restaurant has been making food since 1985, although the bar preceded the restaurant. From the outside on Chambers Street, there's nary a hint of a tiny restaurant hidden inside the windowless building.

Di Salvo & Brennan's on Brady

728 East Brady Street
271-9475
Lower East Side
Dinner Tuesday - Sunday
Smoking in the bar only
Full bar
MC, V, AE
Dress: nicely, wear your gold jewelry

– italian especially sicilian –

T he sun-baked colors of Sicily dominate this restaurant, both outside and in. Puccini from the sound system sets the stage in this intimate restaurant, located at the site formerly occupied by Beyond the Sea. The former Di Salvo's on East Belleview was a cozy space, albeit tiny, and on Brady the owners have kept that intimate feeling by dividing the bar and the eating area, and allowing extra space between tables. They doubled the number of tables, but kept the home cooking that brought patrons again and again to their former location.

This is a family business that goes back to 1966, when the family came to Milwaukee from near Palermo, Sicily with just a few suitcases. Twenty years later they opened a pizzeria but that was shortsighted, for soon they knew they wanted to include Mom Di Salvo's fantastic red sauce, sister Anna's salad dressing and brother Dominic's unusual spiedini. They serve pasta in bowls so the abundant sauce won't spill onto the tablecloth, and the edge forms a platform for soaking the last drop of sauce into your bread.

Prices range from $9.95 for Penne Bolognese to $17.95 for Dominic's Spiedini and $19.95 for Cioppino, seafood simmered with fresh tomatoes and herbs. Salads are a la carte and include the Della Casa, or house salad, for $3.95.

East Garden

3600 North Oakland Avenue
962-7460
Shorewood
Lunch buffet Sunday - Friday
Dinner every day
Smoking - yes, in a separate room
Full bar
MC, V, AE, checks ok
Dress: family style

You will live all the days of your life.

– chinese –

East Garden has received so many congratulations from the critics since they opened in 1982, that to compliment them seems redundant. They serve consistently fresh ingredients in a variety of flavors with an artist's attention to presentation. They can't be perfect however, and our reviewers found a tiny flaw: the fortune cookies had boring fortunes! Worse yet, two people at the table had the same fortune, "You will live all the days of your life." The decor can best be described as Chinese generic with Asian paintings on the walls and a round brick entrance that serves as an unusual focal point from the street.

The food is truly extraordinary, and Szechwan Style Shrimp illustrates the chef's artistry. The hot spicy sauce covering the generous serving of shrimp is bright red, in sharp contrast to crisp, steamed, very green broccoli. It tastes as good as it looks. The Scallops with Garlic Sauce could use a few more scallops to replace some of the abundant water chestnuts, but the overall blended flavors more than make up for the scallop shortage. All the red menu items are "hot and spicy," and a good way to cool the resulting hot lips is with a Tsing Tao beer.

Eddy's Place

1943 North Farwell Avenue
271-9801
Lower East Side
Lunch and dinner Tuesday - Friday
Dinner Saturday and Sunday
Smoking - yes
Bar - yes
Bring cash
Dress: a sarong

– chinese, cantonese –

The decor indoors and out at Eddy's Place is basic, lower East Side anti-chic. But that's part of what brings locals to this eatery, where the vegetables are market fresh and the meat is always tender. Eddy doesn't cut corners when it comes to quality ingredients, and his love of cooking shows in the meals he prepares for his customers. It's hard to spend more than $10, especially at lunchtime when Egg Foo Yung and chow mein are less than $4, and come with tea, soup, and a fortune cookie. Of note is the sweet and sour, a tasty sauce over chicken, pork, or shrimp covered with a tempura-like batter and deep-fried. The sauce is clear and free of that glazed cornstarch look and taste that so often accompanies a sweet and sour dish at luncheon buffet. There's no buffet at Eddy's Place. Everything is cooked to order. Could that be the reason why the food is so good?

Egg Roll House

1507 South 108th Street
771-3011
West Allis
Lunch and dinner every day (includes daily buffet)
Smoking - yes
Full bar
MC, V
Dress: causal

– chinese –

They do a brisk takeout business, and after sampling several specialties, it's clear why the Egg Roll House is so busy. The interior is bright and cheery, and a popular stop for those who prefer their sweet and sour "all you can eat" style. They offer some interesting lunch combos from $4.50 - $4.95; for example, one special includes Beef Chop Suey, Fried Rice and Egg Foo Yung. They have to live up to the name of the restaurant, thus the egg rolls are especially tasty, filled with more meat than greens. All the portions are oversized, and all report that absolutely everything is top drawer.

El Tondero

2462 South 13th Street
384-8835
South Side
Dinner Tuesday - Saturday
Sunday 1:00 p.m. - 5:00 p.m.
Smoking - no
Full bar
MC, V
Dress: not fancy but nice

– peruvian –

For the record, even though El Tondero sounds like a Mexican restaurant, it's not. Peruvian food is quite different from anything one would find in local Mexican restaurants; after all, the countries are separated by Central America and the Panama Canal. Since much of the populated area of Peru is by the sea, one might expect several creative seafood dishes on the menu.

Start with Pescado Al Vapor, a 10-ounce white meat ocean fish fillet, steamed and cooked in Peruvian red-hot sauce. Or try Saltado de Mariscos, seafood served in a red sauce flavored with cilantro. If you're in the mood for a stew, Estofado de Carne o de Pollo, cooked in red wine sauce, is an excellent choice for the less adventuresome who prefer their food not so spicy. Although I haven't tried it, the Sudado De Mariscos was recommended. It's steamed scallops, octopus, squid, conch, shrimp, and mussels cooked in a hot red wine sauce, served with white rice and boiled potatoes. The chicken selections are delicious and so is the Pisco Sour, a drink made with white Peruvian brandy. Don't come to El Tondero if you're in a hurry; everything is made to order!

Estrella

722 East Burleigh Street
264-1863
Riverwest
Lunch and dinner every day
Smoking - no
Bar - beer and Mexican drinks
MC, V, AE
Dress: in lively colors

– mexican, oaxacan –

Here's a charming small Mexican restaurant with a colorful interior; painted ceilings, floor, and walls are all brightly colored and reminiscent of dozens of small restaurants I've visited in Mexico. The menu offers both traditional and regional Oaxacan dishes. The Cream of Chili Poblano soup was a surprise, more heat that I expected, but after a few sips, the exquisite flavors came through, and two slices of bread took the edge off the heat. Instead of heartburn, it left a warm glow.

In place of a lunchtime sandwich, I ordered the dinner appetizer special du jour, a quesadilla cut into eight wedges filled with black beans and goat cheese. "If you don't like goat cheese, try something else," the waitperson suggested. I found it delicious, especially when dipped in the salsa verde, a light mild green salsa that perfectly complemented the flavors and calmed the goat cheese.

White cloth tablecloths, blue cloth napkins, votive candles and romantic Mexican music set a perfect stage for an idyllic south-of-the-border dinner.

Fiesta Garibaldi

8412 West Morgan Avenue
543-4939
West Allis
Lunch and dinner every day
Full bar
Non smoking area
MC, V, AE
Dress: casual

– mexican –

This restaurant is named after Garibaldi Square in Mexico City. Owners Jose Rebollar and Baldemar Escobar hope to please patrons with a combination of Tex-Mex entrees, such as the common taco, tostada, enchilada, burrito or chimichanga, with more traditional Mexican meals for more adventuresome diners. So order a margarita or a tropical drink and float off to someplace south of the border with an authentic Mexican dinner.

The menu helpfully offers pictures of the appetizers and entrees. A whole red snapper from the coast would be a fine choice, or shrimp from the sea served with garlic butter, or perhaps a boneless chicken breast with a Oaxacan mole. Steak served with rice and beans would take you far away to a land of sunshine and mariachi music.

The owners added a children's menu that includes grilled cheese and a cheeseburger in hopes of enticing families to pay a visit to Fiesta Garibaldi. For people unaccustomed Mexican food, this is a good opportunity to try a Tex-Mex meal first, before working up to something more unusual.

Five and Ten Tap

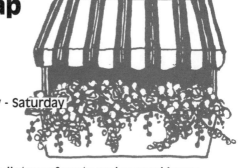

1850 North Water Street
272-1599
Lower East Side
Lunch and dinner Tuesday - Saturday
Smoking - yes
Full bar
Bring cash
Dress: three piece suits, bulletproof vests and ragged jeans
   at noon

– pub food –

Watch customers arrive at this inconspicuous Water Street bar in Town Cars, black Cadillacs, occasionally one with a chauffeur, and hippie vans. To find the Five and Ten, drive north on Water Street past the intersection with Brady Street, veer left, watch for oncoming traffic on Brady, and just past Hamilton Street you'll see the bar across from the former Gallun Tannery. The Tap, tucked into the side of a hill, looks from the outside as if it belongs in Austria instead of downtown Milwaukee. Window boxes filled with red geraniums, and a classy exterior hint of their good food.

At lunch, waitresses perform a juggling act flipping burgers on a grill behind the bar, serving customers at tables and tending the bar. They're impressively efficient; everything comes straight off the grill, no fast food heat lamps here.

In addition to the usual pub food, the Five and Ten offers a fish fry every day for $6.25 and ½ fried chicken every day but Friday for $4.95.

Food-A-Faire

4170 North Oakland Avenue
332-9942
Shorewood
Lunch and dinner Monday - Friday
Saturday close at 3:00 p.m.
Smoking - no
Bar - no
Bring cash
Dress: optional, it's carryout

– fine sandwiches to go –

This deli doesn't win any awards for décor, but who cares? The sandwiches are delicious, always made to order, and the cook isn't in a hurry to slap it together. You'll find a few tables if you want to eat in but why not order a box lunch that includes a sandwich, salad, and a cookie or a muffin or a piece of fruit and take it to the park? Their chocolate chunk cookie is one of the best cookies in the universe, a classic chocolate chip with chunks of dark, semi-sweet, and white chocolate baked into a buttery batter. Each day brings a new lunch special: Cajun Meatloaf on Whole Wheat, Mediterranean Muffuletta, and Grilled Eggplant to name a few.

This family-run cafe also has a kids' menu featuring pb & j grilled or not. The Friday fish fry includes coleslaw, rye bread, and fries or potato pancakes.

The Fork Cafe

W61 N497 Washington Avenue
375-9722
Cedarburg
Lunch Tuesday - Friday
Breakfast and lunch Saturday and Sunday
Dinner on weekends
Smoking - no
Bar - beer (full liquor license coming soon)
MC, V, AE
Dress: preppie

– take-out by day... new american fusion by night –

I try not to get too excited about new restaurants, but The Fork is truly memorable. After starting as caterers, Affairs of the Fork, the owners recently opened this cafe in the heart of Cedarburg. Chef Magister, California trained, is an artist combining flavors, textures and colors. Her presentation is impeccable, her menus creative, and her prices too reasonable. Breakfasts are sublime; nineteen of us from the Walking and Eating Society enjoyed Eggs Benedict and somehow, with no obvious problems, the chef and her helpers served thirty-eight perfectly done eggs on toasted English muffins covered with a melt-in-your-mouth hollandaise sauce. Accompanied by roasted potatoes and fruit salad marinated in key lime juice flavored with coconut and sprinkled with poppy seeds, this was an impressive breakfast. Even the dark roast coffee was especially good.

The Grilled Vegetables on Focaccia with Mozzarella and Roasted Garlic is a meal fit for a celebration, and if one orders the cup of soup and half sandwich, this combo is more than enough for a meal. Soups du jour were Roasted Eggplant, Chilean Chicken Stew, and Wild Rice and Squash, each a culinary achievement not easily replicated in an ordinary kitchen. When the word gets out, a table at The Fork will definitely be worth a wait.

Fortune Chinese Restaurant

639 West Layton Avenue
769-1111
South Side
Lunch and dinner every day
Smoking - yes
Full bar
MC, V, AE
Dress: something loose and casual

– chinese –

Three brothers from Hong Kong own the Fortune Chinese Restaurant, an authentic restaurant where the trick is to get the best food and the secret, ask for the Chinese menu. Thankfully it's bilingual. Under appetizers, instead of egg rolls or Chinese fried chicken, you'll find items such as Jellyfish, Chicken Feet Cantonese Style, or Soyed Cuttlefish. There are twenty-five soups, twenty vegetable and tofu dishes, fifteen rice and noodle dishes, and five egg dishes. Then there's pork, chicken, seafood and beef. Some of the more exotic include Duck Feet with Chinese Mushroom in Casserole, Steamed Minced Pork with Dry Squid, Sautéed Conch with Ginger and Scallion, and Beef Tripe with Black Bean Sauce.

There are two separate dining rooms, a simple one for lunch where you can get a good buffet for $4.95 that varies every day and includes items from the Chinese menu, and a more elegant dining room for evening with tablecloths and flowers.

On weekends they serve Dim Sum from 11:00 a.m. to 3:00 p.m., where you can order from a choice of 25-30 special items priced from $1.50 - $2.50. Be prepared to be adventurous and you won't be disappointed when you order Pork Stomach with Chinese Braising Sauce or Pan Fried Turnip Cake.

Fritz's on Second

814 South Second Street
383-3211
Walker's Point
Lunch and dinner every day
Smoking - yes
Full bar
MC, V, AE
Dress: casual

– pub food - some Cajun –

It used to be called the 2nd Street Saloon. Owner Mike Fritz gutted the interior, turned it into a charming turn-of-the-century bar, and then moved next door to have more space, and did the whole rehab thing all over again. In the process, he gained interior space but lost the outdoor deck.

From the kitchen one can order many different kinds of sandwiches or burgers, all served on oversized buns with fries or salad. The chef makes a thick seafood jambalaya and on Fat Tuesdays they feature Cajun food such as Blackened Pork, Seafood Gumbo, and of course that jambalaya.

A glass-door cabinet features dozens of hot sauces and choosing a sauce for one's sandwich is half the fun of coming to Fritz's. Watch out for the hot ones - it's good to read labels carefully before splashing any sauce on your food. You ordered it - you eat it - hot or otherwise!

Fritz's Pub

3086 South 20th Street
643-6995
South Side
Lunch and dinner every day
Smoking - yes
Full bar
MC, V, AE
Dress: baseball cleats in the summertime

– pub food and serbian specials –

In this unpretentious pub close to the Kinnickinnick Parkway (in case you want to walk off your meal) you'll find the best burger in town. They call it the Serbian Burger, and it's surely not the dieter's special, from the half pound of beef and veal, to the oversized French bread bun, grilled in butter, to the fries served alongside.

Serbian entrees come from the Djuric family history. Mom and Dad came to Milwaukee from Yugoslavia and brought their recipes with them. The menu lists Burek, Shish-Ka-Bob, Chewaps and that phenomenal Serbian Burger. Chicken soup comes from forty pounds of chicken, carrots, onions, celery and spices, simmered for six hours, strained and finished with kluski noodles and sautéed mushrooms. A French chef in a 3-star restaurant in Provence couldn't make better chicken soup.

Save room for dessert. Sister Maria makes a variety of cheesecakes, carrot cake, apple-cranberry pie, and at Christmas, peach cookies that melt in your mouth. There's more. Fritz's Pub serves only homemade bread, and Maria bakes sourdough, wheat, and rye bread daily.

Gil's Cafe

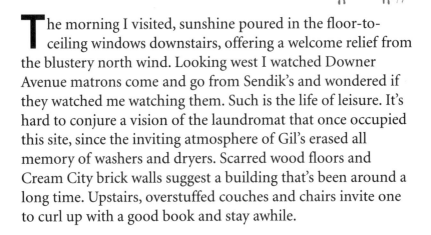

2608 North Downer Avenue
964-4455
Lower East Side
Breakfast, lunch and dinner every day - hours vary
Smoking - no
Bar - no
MC, V
Dress: Downer Avenue chic or UWM tweedy

– cafe food –

The morning I visited, sunshine poured in the floor-to-ceiling windows downstairs, offering a welcome relief from the blustery north wind. Looking west I watched Downer Avenue matrons come and go from Sendik's and wondered if they watched me watching them. Such is the life of leisure. It's hard to conjure a vision of the laundromat that once occupied this site, since the inviting atmosphere of Gil's erased all memory of washers and dryers. Scarred wood floors and Cream City brick walls suggest a building that's been around a long time. Upstairs, overstuffed couches and chairs invite one to curl up with a good book and stay awhile.

Owner Michael Rasmussen, "Gil" came to the coffeehouse business by way of the Culinary Institute of America. Thus one might expect the food to be above average, and it is. The "signature" dishes are especially delicious. Try the Sweet Red Onion Pizza or the Provencal, made with many herbs from Provence in a pesto tomato sauce base covered with layers of goat cheese, fontina and mozzarella. Gil wants to communicate some of the ethnic diversity that makes Milwaukee unique through his food, so he'll mix Italian, French, Greek and Mexican in his unusual menu. His restaurant was mentioned in a 1995 article in the *New York Times*, one of five restaurants the NYT writer found to be especially interesting.

The Great National Saloon & Restaurant

6833 West National Avenue
774-0042
West Allis
Lunch and dinner Monday - Friday
Dinner Saturday
No smoking in the restaurant
Full bar - good selection of non-alcoholic wine
MC, V, AE
Dress: business suits at lunch, anything goes at dinner
(might need an expanding elastic waistband)

Im Lieben übermächtig, Das ist die deutsche Art.

– gourmet continental –

Former owners Rosemary and Jerry Trasser turned the back room of a neighborhood saloon into a memorable restaurant. This ballroom-turned-restaurant dates back to the 1920s and has hosted many rollicking parties. In the past, a concertina band played on a raised area in a back corner. When the downtown Embers Steakhouse closed, the Trassers bought the interior fixtures, including leaded glass and carved wood panels, and installed them in the dining room, creating an inviting atmosphere loaded with historical charm.

Here's a clear example of the reason this book was written. Neighborhood restaurants like the Great National Saloon & Restaurant take us back to Old Milwaukee. Their owners demonstrate the historic importance of taking pride in reasonably priced, quality food, well prepared, and presented in an inviting atmosphere.

Visit on a Tuesday or Thursday and try the rib special for $7.95. It's an "all you can eat" offer, but the portions are already generous and most can barely finish the first helping, served with garlic mashed potatoes and broccoli.

Harry's Bar and Grille

3549 North Oakland Avenue
964-6800
Shorewood
Lunch and dinner every day
Smoking - yes
Full bar
MC, V, AE
Dress: power suits to jeans

– high class pub food –

The first time I walked into Harry's Bar and Grille, I followed two elderly women into the bar. A preconceived stereotype bit the dust as I realized Harry's caters to an eclectic crowd, not just the North Shore business set who drop by for a power lunch and an after work martini. A friend from Illinois and I came at 1:00 p.m. on a weekday to enjoy a late lunch, and as we talked at our table next to the floor-to-ceiling windows, I could almost forget this is Milwaukee and not Manhattan or Chicago's Lincoln Park. The turn of the century buildings across the street added another dimension to Harry's as the sun illuminated the street scene.

The same people who own and manage Harry's also own the North Shore Bistro and The Knickerbocker Cafe downtown. They have a handle on how to keep the cash flow and customers coming, and this is meant as compliment. The food is excellent at neighborhood-reasonable prices to lure regulars to stop often for more than just a quick drink.

Don't miss the Grilled Vegetable Sandwich with strips of eggplant, zucchini, tomato, and red onion on herb focaccia bread with basil oil. Likewise, we recommend the signature dish, Stack-O' Potatoes; fried Idaho and sweet potatoes stuffed with black bean puree, diced tomato, onion, lettuce, and cheese served with sour cream and guacamole.

Hector's

7118 North State Street
258-5600
Wauwatosa
Lunch and dinner every day
Open at 3:00 p.m. on Sunday
Smoking - yes
Full bar
MC, V, checks ok
Dress: colorful

– mexican –

These relative newcomers serve delicious Mexican food west of Walker's Point, the center of Milwaukee's south-of-the-border population. Wauwatosans appreciate a good dish of guacamole and chips too, and at Hector's they don't scrimp on the portions. Of note is Chicken Mole served with flour tortillas and the usual rice and beans. They bone the chicken and simmer generous chunks in a spicy traditional mole sauce prepared with a tomato base, chilies, sweet cocoa, peanut butter and spices. You can buy mole sauce in a jar at Mercado El Rey and fix it at home, but it's more fun to let Hector's cook the mole so you can scoop it up with tortillas and watch the crowd. Another reviewer's favorite is Chili Relleno, a pepper filled with cheese, coated with an egg batter, sautéed, and served with a generous covering of tomato sauce. For light appetites, this one's not as filling as some of the other specials.

Henry's

2523 East Belleview
332-9690
Lower East Side
Dinner every day
Smoking – yes
Bar – yes, it *is* a bar!
MC, V, AE
Dress: trendy

– bar food –

Henry's was displaced when the Coffee Trader complex disappeared, but they soon resurfaced around the corner at the former location of Cafe di Salvo, now located on Brady Street and renamed Di Salvo and Brennen. You may recall the Cafe was tiny; so is Henry's, with fewer than a dozen tables and a bar. That's all there is. To their credit, location is everything, and they're right around the corner from the Downer Theater. That's key for people who like to combine a meal and a movie. The burgers are fine, so are the fries. If you order the meat medium-rare, be prepared, it could be surprisingly rare.

Hi-Fi Cafe

2640 South Kinickinick
486-0504
Bayview
Breakfast, lunch and dinner every day
Smoking - no
Bar - no
Bring cash
Dress: cafe casual

– market fresh salads and sandwiches –

This is the site of the former Casablanca at the corner of KK and Potter in Bayview. Also at this corner, across the street, sits a very fancy McDonalds where, might I suggest, the food isn't market-fresh. At the Hi-Fi Cafe *everything* is fresh and you can trust the menu to deliver what's promised.

During the week they serve breakfast until 11:00 a.m.; that's what brought me the first time, but 11:00 means just that and breakfast is over at 11:15. However, the person who sent me here raved about the omelets, especially spinach-feta served with toasted French bread. My late breakfast turned into an early lunch and the Cheese Muffalata did not disappoint. If you order the sandwich on a baguette, bring a bib! Lettuce and sliced red onion come flying out at every bite, but not to worry, there's plenty of provolone cheese and olive pepper salad hiding underneath to give it a delicious flavor. Fresh herbs appeared in both the accompanying pasta salad and the sandwich, a nice touch.

They also serve a variety of salads, homemade pizza, a couple of soup choices, and a mouth-watering selection of hot and cold drinks.

The Highlander

5921 West Vliet
479-0620
Milwaukee, close to Washington Highlands
Lunch and dinner Monday - Friday
Dinner Saturday
Smoking - yes
Bar - yes
MC, V, AE
Dress: anything goes

– pub food –

C an you imagine a restaurant or bar that has a television but doesn't turn it on? Not even during important games! And yet they survive as a popular bar / restaurant, a neighborhood gathering place. Instead of TV noise, they play an eclectic choice of background music from Billie Holliday to Eric Clapton to instrumental jazz.

The Highlander serves the usual burgers, plus a veggie burger and a fabulous grilled portabella mushroom sandwich. The only time one has to wait for a table is on Friday, when everyone turns out for the popular fish fry. However, during the warm months, the new deck takes the pressure off the small dining area.

If it's your habit to combine dinner and a movie, then it's good to know that The Highlander is across Vliet from the Times Theater.

Hi Hat Lounge

Corner Brady Street and Arlington Place
225-9330
Lower East Side
Lounge menu every day 4:00 p.m. - 2:00 a.m.
Sunday Brunch 10:00 a.m. - 3:00 p.m.
Smoking - yes (in the lower bar area)
Full bar
MC, V, AE
Dress: trendy

– fancy "lounge food" and haute cuisine brunch –

It took a dreary day to entice me to this restaurant. Instead of a walk, we opted for breakfast at the Hi Hat. With no expectations, we wandered in the rain to the Brady Street locale at about 10:30 on a Sunday. We were just in time to be seated before the late breakfast crowd started to arrive, and by the time we left about noon, every table was taken and people were waiting. When breakfast came, we knew why the Hi Hat was so popular. "What's good?" I had asked our waitress and she replied, " Shrimp and Grits," and that's what I ordered. The shrimp were cooked to perfection, slightly spicy, served in a white wine sauce with sun-dried tomatoes, leeks and garlic over cheese grit cakes that held their flavor without competing with the spicy sauce.

Green Eggs and Ham, with all due respect to Dr Seuss, turned out to be another winner. A spin-off from traditional eggs benedict, the chef layered ham, poached eggs and a fresh chive aioli on toasted English muffins. Don't order it unless you like garlic; perhaps they should have named the sauce "garlic-chive aioli."

Most breakfast entrees come with sweet potato hash, a mix of sweet potatoes and red potatoes seasoned with fresh rosemary, but instead of fried or oven-baked potatoes, this hash was made with steamed potatoes,eliminating the oil that usually accompanies breakfast potatoes.

Hong Thai Restaurant

6501 West Greenfield Avenue
257-9114
West Allis
Lunch and dinner Monday - Friday
Dinner only Saturday
Smoking - yes
Small bar
MC, V, AE
Dress: a sarong?

– thai –

The jury's hung on Hong Thai. Some like it, some don't. Those who do think the food is excellent, the waitstaff eager to please, and the Asian music a perfect background accompaniment. Those who don't, found the service and restrooms marginal, the food average and the sauces delicious!

On the plus side, the Thai Spring Rolls served with homemade plum sauce are a treat, as is Tom Yum Gai soup nicely seasoned with lemongrass, and Pudt Cashew Nuts, a perfect mix of chicken, nuts, peppers, scallions, and mushrooms served in a sweet sauce.

The owner Noudeum Pophananouvong came to Milwaukee from Laos not Thailand, nevertheless he kept Pudt Thai, a dish some call Thailand's national food, on the menu. One will oft find it prepared by street vendors in Bangkok or Chaing Mai and no matter where it's done, it's always tasty. As in Thailand, at Hong Thai, it's inexpensive, delicious, and filling.

Hooligans

2017 East North Avenue
273-5230
Lower East Side
Lunch and dinner Monday - Saturday
Smoking - yes
Full bar
MC, V
Dress: by weekday business casual, evenings trendy

– bar food –

On that crazy corner where Farwell, North, Murray and Ivanhoe Place meet, Hooligans is the skinny triangular shaped bar facing west on North Avenue. Close to the Oriental Theater, it's a popular place all day and well into the evening, after the food service has closed at 10:00 p.m. After all, it's first a bar and second a restaurant, though that's not quite the case when one studies the lengthy six page menu or tries one of their sandwiches. Hooligan's has been around since 1936 and times have changed from the days when a bar was a bar, just a place to pound down the drinks.

The menu has an entire page devoted to chicken sandwiches, starting with a naked Grilled Breast of Chicken and getting progressively more impressive, when a daily special lists Sacramento Chicken with Bacon, grilled chicken breast with avocado hollandaise and lemon-peppered bacon.

In fact, the daily specials, Monday - Friday are all on the creative side of sandwiches, and someone in the kitchen must be having fun designing these menus. How about Cats and Cakes, seasoned grilled catfish filet served atop Creole rice cakes and topped with remoulade. Did I say "bar food?"

Hotel Metro

411 East Mason Street
272-1937
Downtown
Breakfast, lunch and dinner every day
Full bar
Smoking - no
MC, V, AE
Dress: nicely

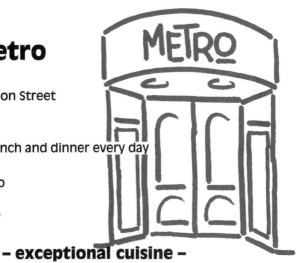

– exceptional cuisine –

This is a restaurant where dinner is out of the price range for this book, but since their breakfast is such a delicious treat, it's a shame not to give the Hotel Metro restaurant a mention. Both the hotel and the restaurant are done in Art Deco style, with everything made to order. Notice the Tibetan hand-woven rug in the reception area, and while you're looking at floors, notice the bamboo floor. The rooms are as beautiful as is the lobby, and one has a hard time picturing the hotel's former occupant, a brokerage business.

Breakfast is a quiet affair on weekdays, with few other diners and a large dining room to cushion table talk. The Eggs Florentine, two poached eggs on toasted English muffin halves with sautéed spinach, cheddar cheese sauce, fresh fruit garnish and red potatoes, is everything it promises. Perfectly done eggs covered with a light cheese sauce sit on top of a generous serving of fresh spinach. For people who love Eggs Benedict but don't want the calories, this is a fine substitute. The Irish oatmeal brulee is another extraordinary breakfast choice, recommended by several friends. The coffee is strong, the service excellent and they won't rush you to move along so they can resell your table. A fine place for a morning romance.

ICC Ristorante

631 East Chicago Street
223-2185
Third Ward
Lunch Monday - Friday
Dinner Monday - Saturday
Closed Sunday
Smoking - yes
Bar - yes
MC, V
Dress: gold chains optional

- italian -

This is not a lowbrow community center restaurant, where the food is canned, and "if it's Monday, it's meatballs and marinara." Daily specials are posted in the dining room, and for the quantity and quality of the food, one won't find a better place for lunch or dinner in Milwaukee. And, in the summer on a warm evening, the outside patio is a delight, and seldom crowded.

An unusual lunch sandwich is the Steak Prosciutto, grilled tenderloin topped with prosciutto, roasted red peppers, tomatoes and provolone cheese. On an ordinary day, lunch specials might include Cajun Shrimp Caesar Salad, Pesto Tortellini with Mushrooms and Tomatoes, Chicken Walnut over Rice, Steak Dijon with Pesto Tortellini, and Havana Chicken over Barbequed Black Beans.

Order from the appetizer menu at night, Cheese and Fruit Plate, and a Focaccia Pizza, and you have enough for a dinner for two. Spinach and Asiago Chicken belongs in the finest of restaurants and the price is very reasonable for this whole boned chicken breast covered with fresh spinach and melted Asiago cheese.

Jake's

6030 West North Avenue
771-0550
Wauwatosa
Dinner daily (hours vary)
Smoking - no!!!
Full bar
MC, V, checks ok
Dress: doesn't matter, they have dim separate booths, most
    dress up

– steak house –

OK - it's a steak house, and they're famous for their steak, twice baked potato, and onion rings "eat till you explode" feeding frenzy, but to stay inside a $10 limit (well close), please visit Jake's on Friday. The fish fry, expensive by Milwaukee's low budget Friday fry standards, is a bargain here. Since you'll probably wait 45 minutes to an hour in the bar, they provide sustenance for faint-hearted TGIF patrons. A pecan-filled cheese dip served with crackers and bagel chips will soften a tummy rumble until you get into a private booth in the dining area. Then they immediately present you with two round steaming loaves of homemade bread. There are several choices to accompany the baked or deep-fried haddock, including creamed spinach with a hint of nutmeg, coleslaw filled with red and green cabbage and bits of pineapple, and Jake's famous onion rings. All are highly recommended by our reviewers.

The waitresses are friendly and quick to refill a half-full water glass. They encourage a final gluttonous fling at the dessert tray, and why not after indulging in cheese dip, buttery bagel chips, creamed spinach and deep fried onion rings? The Key Lime Pie, made on the premises with limes from southern Florida, is just the right combination of tart and sweet. Or for a final sweet ending, try the melt-in-your-mouth chocolate mousse.

Jake's Deli

1634 West North Avenue
562-1272
Central city, Near North Side
Lunch Monday - Saturday
Smoking - yes
Beer only
No credit, no checks, bring cash!
Dress: wash and wear, your sandwich will drip

– deli –

Jake's has been around Milwaukee peddling Kosher-style corned beef for eighty-three years. A series of owners dates back to the original location at 7th and Walnut. Jake himself worked for the first owners Guten and Cohen, bought them out, eventually sold the operation to local businessmen, and today son Mike runs the business.

This is the place for a good corned beef sandwich. They pile 1½ inches of meat onto light rye, lay a slice of Swiss cheese on top, and serve it with a pickle. Count on lean beef here where quality ranks along with quantity. Jake's isn't very big, just a few wooden booths, a few tables and a five-stool counter in case they get busy. They call a chicken a chicken and specialize in chicken noodle and chicken rice soups along with matzo ball soup and cabbage-rich borsch. Don't fret if you forget your calculator. A prominent sign list prices for one - ten sandwiches and that applies to corned beef, pastrami and tongue. A poster-size sign explains, "no refunds given without return of merchandise."

Jalapeño Loco

4905 South Packard Avenue
483-8300
Cudahy
Lunch and dinner Tuesday - Sunday
Smoking - yes
Full bar
MC, V
Dress: anything goes here

– mexican –

This cozy bar-restaurant in Cudahy serves both the usual Tex-Mex entrees and a selection of specialties not usually found in local Mexican restaurants. Whatever one orders, the service is fast and friendly, the food is well prepared and it's always served hot. Reviewers raved about the Mole Oaxaqueno and the Sautéed Chicken with Poblano Salsa Gratinada, both listed on a note board on the restaurant's north wall. Mole is a common Mexican menu item in Milwaukee and Oaxacan mole, from the city of that name, will usually be a rich dark concoction. This mole was red and covered chunks of chicken white meat instead of the common mole served on the bone – this way you get more chicken and it's all tender white meat.

Adventuresome diners will want to check the board before ordering from the printed menu. Jalapeño Loco serves some of the most exciting Mexican entrees found on local menus. Don't miss Chiles en Nogadas, stuffed peppers with walnut sauce.

Jalisco's

2207 East North Avenue
291-0645
Lower East Side
Breakfast, lunch and dinner every day
Smoking - yes
Full bar
MC, V
Dress: serape optional, especially when the band plays on
    weekends

– mexican –

You won't be disappointed by this East Side Mexican eatery. A string of restaurants has popped up and sunk again at this location, but Jalisco's could be the one that stays. The decor will take you back to that cafe in Tijuana, the one with the horns, piñatas, flags, stuffed parrots, serapes and pottery decorating the walls. All you need is a mariachi band playing outside in the street for a scene straight from old Mexico.

Settle in with a Dos Equis or lemonade and enjoy cheap, authentic Mexican food. When they say hot, they mean "hot." Keeping this in mind, I recommend the Chicken Mole.

Since they're open for breakfast, it's a good place to have huevos rancheros and rice and beans in the morning. Jalisco's could easily be in Mexico but it's here on Milwaukee's East Side, close to the Oriental Theater and a handy apres-movie snack stop.

Jerry's Old Town Inn

N116 W15841 Main Street
251-4455
Germantown
Dinner every day
Sunday 4:00 - 7:00 p.m.
Smoking - not in the main dining room
Full bar
MC, V
Dress: up

– home cooking, famous for BBQ ribs –

OK - Jerry's is a bit out of the way for people who don't live northwest of Milwaukee, but it's well worth the trip for a special dinner. My first impression of Jerry's came when I called to make a Friday night reservation and a voice with a smile asked, "How many in your party?" When we arrived our table was ready, yet when we lingered over an appetizer and after dinner coffee there wasn't a hint of "hurry up, we have a group waiting."

The restaurant was originally a bed and breakfast, located close to the train depot, and it housed passengers who traveled to Germantown on the train. The food is exemplary and the portions more than a person can eat at one sitting. For example the Beer Battered Cod came with a choice of soup du jour, a salad, homemade bread, and a choice of potatoes. At dinner I choose Seafood Chowder, a fork-thick white chowder, German Potato salad with abundant bacon bits and a delicious sweet and sour dressing, both served with homemade rye bread. Four pieces of cod and I needed a doggie bag!

The ribs need no introduction. Jerry's is famous for them and if you can put away a 32-ounce portion, you can join the "Clean Plate Club."

Joe's Cafe

3519 West Silver Spring
461-0210
Northwest Side
Breakfast, lunch and dinner Monday - Friday
Smoking - yes
No bar
Bring cash
Dress: working class

– diner food –

I heard about Joe's on a flight home from Montana. The source was good; a former food salesman who called on the cafe and insisted a visit wouldn't be complete without meeting the legendary Josafa Platzer. He was right. She calls almost every person who walks into her restaurant by name. Customers sit at one of four tables or at a counter that seats a dozen, and a short wait for a table only proves the popularity of Joe's place.

Each day there's a different special. For example, Joe will cook Swiss steak, a breaded and fried steak that's baked in a combination tomato sauce and beef gravy, and serve it with real mashed potatoes, Harvard beets and a roll. Other specials include meat loaf, tenderloin tips, beef stew, and breaded pork chops. This isn't fancy food but it's good, always homemade, never reheated, and made with the finest ingredients.

When customers wait outside the front door at 5:00 a.m., something is right. Joe says 85% of her customers are regulars. Maybe her homemade jellies lure them back. Joe harvests fruit from her backyard, customers bring her their bounty and she cooks jelly all year long for the cafe.

Johnny's Club Carnival

2394 South Kinnickinnic
744-5810
Bayview
Breakfast, lunch and dinner every day
Smoking - yes
Full bar
MC
Dress: jeans

– mexican –

These neighborhood restaurants come to me by word of mouth and Johnny's is a last-minute addition, thanks to a friend who used to be a semi-regular. It's been a bar for a very long time, and in the recent past, the owner opened an adjoining restaurant where food is served all day, every day of the week. The Beftic al la Mexicana and the Beftic Milanesa, both $7, are served in typical Mexican style, cut from the steak across instead of vertically. A la Mexicana, strips marinated and served with a spicy sauce, is a great choice as is the Milanesa, a breaded fried steak. Camarones a la Plancha, grilled shrimp with rice and salad is a popular entree as is shrimp stew with vegetables.

The most popular night is Tuesday when three enchiladas, rice and beans are just $4. On Friday the fish fry is cod or cat and shrimp enchiladas are also available only on Friday.

Breakfast, served from 8:00 a.m. to 11:00 a.m., includes the popular Mexican Chilaquiles as well as Menudo or tripe, an acquired taste in the a.m.

Kegel's

5901 West National Avenue
257-9999
West Allis
Lunch Monday - Friday
Dinner Monday - Saturday
Smoking - yes in the bar
Full bar
MC, V, AE
Dress: dress up or down, you'll fit in

– german –

Grandpa Kegel opened this look-alike Old World German rathskeller in 1924. Today you can sit at one of the wooden tables and almost hear Milwaukee's German immigrants, boisterous and merry, singing a rowdy drinking song. Beer flowed here discreetly during Prohibition. They brewed it in the basement, hiding this covert operation behind a fake wall. Yes, they were busted once or twice, but the money and the beer kept flowing. When Prohibition ended in 1933, Grandpa Kegel took the beer money and renovated the restaurant.

The interior is warm and inviting. Everything's wood, including three-quarter inch tongue and groove oak paneled walls and a mahogany bar that's one long slice of tree. The wall paintings above the paneling were done by hand, and the stained glass windows were crafted by Grandpa Kegel's friend Peter Gries.

The food's great too. The best entrees are of course the traditional German selections, but they run a bit above the $10 mark. The Friday fish fry is superb, one of Milwaukee's best. Drop in for a stout German beer and say hello to owners Jim and Bob Kegel.

Koppa's Fulbeli Deli

1940 North Farwell
273-1273
Lower East Side
Open every day, stop making specialty sandwiches at 6:00 p.m.
Smoking - no
Bar - no
Bring cash
Dress: something comfortable

– a grocery store with a sandwich deli –

Jump on Milwaukee's downtown trolley during the summer months and see what's good about Milwaukee, from Brady Street to Water Street to the Third Ward, to museums, parks, and marinas. On Thursdays, plan a picnic at one of the free jazz concerts in Cathedral Square, but first stop at Koppas's Fulbeli Deli before 6:00 p.m. to pick up a sandwich to go with the beer you can buy at the concert.

At Koppa's they make some of the best and the most creative sandwiches I've encountered. My favorites are the Rimpish, shaved ham, shaved turkey, provolone, lettuce, tomatoes, mayo, bacon and secret sauce, all layered on double deck Vienna white bread; the Atlantis, mozzarella, colby, peppers, tomatoes, cucumbers, sprouts, pepperoncini and cranberry mustard rolled into grilled pita bread; and finally Mary, shaved roast beef, Swiss cheese, peppers, onions, lettuce, bourbon mustard, all served on La Boulangerie's super bread. They also have bakery from East Side Ovens and La Bou if you want dessert to complete your picnic in the park.

Kopp's Frozen Custard

5373 North Port Washington Road
961-2006
Whitefish Bay
Lunch and dinner 7 days a week
Smoking - no
No bar
Bring cash
Dress: North Shore chic

– carryout only –

They publish a monthly calendar of the daily custard flavors so thousands of Kopp's fans can plan ahead for Caramel Cashew or Cookies and Cream. Even below zero temperatures don't deter Kopp's custard lovers.

When they say "cashew" they mean "cashews" plural, with many nuts in every spoonful. Cones start at $1.18 for a large single, and peak at $3.70 for six scoops. If you order it in a dish, they garnish your custard with a delicious flaky cookie. A reviewer's comment: "To beat the blues, indulge in a turtle sundae, an orgy of custard, hot fudge and caramel sauces, toasted pecans, and whipped cream topped with a cherry."

Unlike ordinary fast food places, Kopp's cooks everything to order, and the food is well worth the wait. Recently they added skinless grilled chicken breast to the burger menu that also includes the LTM (lettuce, tomato and mayo), a plain breast, and a Mexican inspired Caliente breast with salsa, cheese and jalapeño pepper. Anyone who orders the Buffalo chicken sandwich will want to bring a bib or grab extra napkins. They serve this drippy sandwich on an oversized bun with a spicy blue cheese celery sauce / dressing. It's good. While you wait, you can admire the Claes Oldenburg-style sculpture of a six-foot-tall metal spoon and large bright red cherry set in the middle of the room.

La Boulangerie

241 North Broadway
271-3900
Third Ward
Breakfast, lunch 7 days a week (they close at 6:00 p.m.)
Smoking - no
Bar - no
No credit, checks OK
Dress: downtown upscale mixed with business attire

– continental –

M ost people know La Boulangerie for their morning buns, often served at other establishments. However, they serve the rest of their pastries, along with breakfast and lunch at three locations in metro Milwaukee. All share similar menus. There's a "La Bou" at 1425 Underwood in Wauwatosa, and another on Mequon Road just off I-43 in Mequon. It's not easy to find the Third Ward La Bou. A sign in the window of the Loft Space building leads customers downstairs. It's underneath Gingrass Gallery and Eccola, and next to Aveda. They redecorated the restaurant in 1992 and painted the formerly fire engine red chairs avocado green and the overhead ducts eggplant. Now chairs and pipes match salads and entrees.

On an average day they'll offer eleven different kinds of muffins, including chocolate chip, chocolate chip pumpkin, and double chocolate chip banana for hard core chocophiles. They rotate a colorful selection of fresh salads and display four different menus each week. Daily salads might include Caesar Chicken Salad, Tortellini with Pepperoni Sauce, Winter Couscous, and Spinach with Buttermilk Dressing. They serve cafeteria style and no one minds if customers linger. Art from the Gingrass Gallery decorates the Cream City brick walls lit with track lights. La Bou feels like a combination gallery/cafe that also happens to serve good food. It's trendy, comfortable, popular, and well deserves its reputation for excellence.

La Casita

2014 North Farwell Avenue
277-1177
Lower East Side
Lunch Tuesday - Saturday
Dinner every day
Smoking - only in the bar
Full bar
MC, V, AE
Dress: casual

– mexican-southwestern –

Drive down Farwell Avenue on a summer evening and you'll see standing room only on the deck at this popular restaurant. An imaginative menu that keeps vegetarians happy is one of the secrets of their success. If you're looking for multiple meatless entrees, La Casita is a find.

The black bean cakes served with mesquite-grilled carrots, zucchini, broccoli, and onions and are delicious, as are vegetable fajitas, an unusual version of the traditional chicken or beef.

If you want to go beyond ordinary tacos and tostados, pay La Casita a visit. If you come on a weekend night, be prepared for a wait in the bar, where it can get noisy.

La Fuente

625 South 5th Street
271-8595
Walker's Point
Lunch and dinner every day
Smoking - yes
Full bar
MC, V, AE
Dress: sweatshirts and jeans (jewels worn here)

– mexican –

Even at 5:30 p.m. on a winter Sunday evening, the wait can extend past thirty minutes, but if one is inclined toward a margarita, the bartender here blends the booze well. Maybe this contributes to the decibel level of the table talk; romantic conversation won't work here. Instead, admire the special decor, a fountain scene decorated with Christmas lights. Even without velvet paintings, the owner has kept Mexican kitsch alive at La Fuente.

Once seated, the service is fast and attentive. In fact, so quick that dinner arrived before the reviewers had sufficient time to enjoy their margaritas and munch on chips and pico de gallo. The combo plates are excellent, especially #3, one chimichanga, one enchilada, and one taco. The chef doesn't scrimp on the dollop of guacamole on the side, and the choice of flour or corn tortilla for the taco adds a nice touch. If one chooses a corn tortilla, there is an additional choice of soft or hard.

Overall La Fuente's "authentic Mexican cuisine" offers a fine value at $6.50 for the combo, including rice and beans.

Lakeside Inn

801 North Cass Street
276-1577
Downtown
Breakfast, lunch and dinner every day
Smoking - no
Full bar
MC, V, AE
Dress: funky-upscale-downtown-theater gowns or jeans

– fine dining –

This restaurant-coffee house-bed and breakfast, serves three creative meals a day in a comfortable relaxed setting. The menu boasts, "all entrees are individually prepared," and the meal presentation at the Inn suggests this is indeed true. For the carnivore, Steak Dianne and Champagne Steak are especially tasty. They do an unusual variation of Steak Dianne, and serve it with mushrooms and broccoli along with the traditional cognac and brown sauce. Champagne Steak is truly unique with a combination of capers, smoked salmon, zucchini, rice, and a champagne sauce. Brunch omelets here are legend, and when they offer a Corned Beef Omelet, they stuff it with shredded, sautéed corned beef. Somehow, the chef manages to liposuction the fat so it's all meat.

Lakeside Inn offers an atmosphere of casual elegance with some artsy touches, and muted classical music stimulates both good conversation and a desire to linger over dessert and coffee. Even the chairs are comfortably bent.

They serve fish on a special fish-shaped platter, and their coffee mugs feel like they're meant for serious coffee drinkers. The ambience is Chicago, New York, San Francisco or best of all, downtown Milwaukee!

Lalli's Pizza Carı

8826 West North Avenue
(Adjacent to Club Tap)
774-9838
West Side (Wauwatosa)
Open 4:30 p.m. daily
Checks ok
Dress: home movie casual

– pizza, take-out –

Lalli's closed their Center Street location, but they serve the same menu at Club Tap. It's a separate operation from the bar, but it's the same Lalli's pizza they used to make on Center Street.

Tony Lalli and his partner Pat Brighum know how to make Italian food. With dozens of carryout pizzerias in Milwaukee, Lalli's is the reviewers' choice for a mention in this neighborhood restaurant collection. For an at-home feed and bloat, Italian gourmands start with an order of mozzarella marinara, four pieces of cheese breaded with Lalli's own Italian bread crumbs, deep fried and served with a cup of marinara sauce. Follow with Lalli's Sicilian salad, an array of lettuce, tomato, peppers, olives, mushrooms, and cheese served with house dressing on the side; and finish with the coup de grace, the pizza. When it comes to pizza, there's decent, mediocre, boring, soggy, good, bad, indifferent and Lalli's. We call it sublime. At least in Wauwatosa, why cook? Lalli's is just a phone call away.

La Perla

Corner 5th and National Avenue
645-9888
Walker's Point
Lunch and dinner every day
Smoking - yes
Full bar
MC, V
Dress: a Pancho Villa sombrero and something red to match
   their chilies

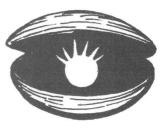

– mexican –

La Perla is hardly a well-kept secret. They started small in a space formerly occupied by another restaurant, and from that inauspicious beginning, La Perla has become a major purveyor of Mexican food in Walker's Point. As their reputation spread, they increased their space, and today they have more than doubled the original restaurant by annexing the adjacent shop and adding a wonderful deck out back. Heaters extend the deck season for intrepid outdoor diners. On a summer evening, this deck is the place to be seen, sipping a margarita and looking cool.

The waitstaff are always cheerful - no matter how busy they are, they'll smile, and the food will put a smile on your face too. Prices are reasonable, especially for a restaurant this trendy, and the most you can spend is $12 for Camarone al Mojo de Ajo, sautéed shrimp with garlic butter. If feeling adventuresome, order a Guadalajara Steak Picado Verde, steak with green sauce, grilled onions and peppers, and you'll leave with a full belly and maybe tomorrow's lunch.

Las Palmas

1901 South 60th
329-9600
South Side
Dinner Monday - Thursday
Lunch and dinner Friday - Sunday
Smoking - yes
Full bar
MC, V, AE
Dress: business suits or skirt and heels, but not at the same
time

– mexican –

Good Mexican restaurants have expanded to areas beyond Walker's Point, popping up all over town. Las Palmas is a good example of a new south-of-the-border style cantina that's left 5th and National and set up shop on 60th Street.

The menu offers few surprises, but the quality of the food is consistently good. My reviewers should know; they too own a restaurant.

The decor is festive Mexican, the music is um-pah mariachi, and just in case one runs out of conversation, the owner's Harley decorates a corner of the dining room. As a counterpoint to this Milwaukee machine, a fountain bubbles in another corner.

The Las Palmas Combination Plato Fuerte is highly recommended. Chicken, steak, and shrimp are sautéed with red and green peppers and onions and served with flour tortillas, pico de gallo, guacamole, and sour cream. Reviewers gave this combo plato a 4-star thumbs up.

Lisa's

2961 North Oakland Avenue
332-6360
East Side
Dinner every day
Smoking - yes
Full bar
MC, V
Dress: jeans

– italian –

Here's another family-run neighborhood restaurant that's survived the fickle public for thirty-five years, making one of the best thin crust pizzas in Milwaukee. My family has feasted on Lisa's Super Pizza for twenty of those thirty-five years, and has seldom left without full tummies and a doggie bag. Super means sausage, mushroom, pepperoni, and green pepper; the $11.50, 14" pizza will easily feed two adults.

For dinner they'll fix spedini, spaghetti, ravioli, chicken cacciatore and lasagne, and toss in a salad with homemade Italian dressing and all the bread you can eat. The chicken cacciatore, boned chicken simmered with peppers and onions, is a favorite. Cooked slowly, the tomato-based sauce absorbs the flavors of the peppers and onions and perfectly complements the generous serving of boned chicken. I give Lisa's A+.

Lopez Bakery

624 West National Avenue
383-4845
Walker's Point
Breakfast, lunch and dinner every day
Smoking - no
Bar - no
Will take checks
Dress: wear a smile, everyone else does

– mexican –

L opez Bakery was featured on the cover of *The Food Lover's Guide to Milwaukee.* As a person who's traveled often to Mexico, I can vouch for the authenticity of the bakery products at Lopez, for their cookies, pastries and breads are better than any I have sampled in my travels in Mexico. Jose Lopez brought his recipes to Milwaukee from San Luis Potosi where he came from a family of bakers, starting with his grandfather. His sons George and Jose are fourth generation bakers.

By the end of 1999 there will be three Lopez bakeries, the original on National Avenue, the second on Lincoln Avenue, and a third to open in 1999 on Mitchell Street. At the National Avenue location, Jose Lopez also operates a small restaurant where they serve a variety of traditional Mexican foods including the tamales Jose's wife Ampara makes for the weekend rush. To make them, she spreads the corn husks with dough made from corn flour, shortening, salt, baking powder, and paprika, then fills them with a pork mixture and steams them for one to two hours. Also on the menu are Huevos Rancheros Con Chorizo or ala Mexicana, Tacos al Pastor, tortas and gorditas.

For Jose and Ampara Lopez this is a dream come true. The bakery/restaurant is the quintessential family business run by Jose, his wife, sons Jose and George, and on the wall, beautiful photos of their grandchildren.

Los Mariachis

4305 West Layton Avenue
325-7800
Greenfield
Lunch and dinner every day
Smoking - yes
Full bar
MC, V
Dress: sombrero, Pancho Villa style

– mexican –

D on't order mayo on a chicken sandwich at Los Mariachis, but then who would order a chicken sandwich at a Mexican restaurant? Instead, wear a serape, come on a weekend night and enjoy the three-piece mariachi band. If you find the large menu overwhelming, ask a waitperson and you'll get a helpful answer, and most likely one that directs you to something more adventuresome than the combo plate, which, by the way, is delicious. The Milwaukee Walking and Eating Society rated Los Mariachis their favorite Mexican restaurant and they all ate the #1 combo plate, a chicken tostada, a chicken taco, and a chicken enchilada. The enchilada was especially tasty with the meat wrapped in a corn tortilla and baked in a tomato chili sauce. All the specials are served with rice and beans. A house special, Pollo Tepic is served on a sizzling platter like the familiar fajitas but with the addition of red and yellow peppers, carrots, and tomatoes. This relatively new (April 1997) restaurant gets thumbs up from 21 reviewers!

Lotus

7236 South 76th
427-7200
Franklin
Lunch and dinner every day
Non-smoking section
Full bar
MC, V, AE
Dress: casual

– chinese –

Lotus isn't exactly a newcomer to the Milwaukee restaurant business, since the original Lotus dates back to the 1970s on Old World Third Street. This Lotus is owned by a nephew of the original owner.

Reviewers especially recommended three dishes: Subgum War BAR Shrimp, beef, chicken, and BBQ pork cooked with vegetables and served on a sizzling platter with a sprinkle of brandy and assorted nuts; Singapore Fried Rice Noodles, rice noodles wok-fried with pork, shrimp, eggs, green peppers, and bean sprouts in a curry based sauce; and Sesame Chicken with Strawberries, fresh orange, and peapods in a light sweet and sour sauce.

If you mouth isn't watering yet, come for the BBQ Pork-Fried Rice, the best fried rice this side of San Francisco's Chinatown. So many tastes - so little time!!!

Lynne's Kitchen

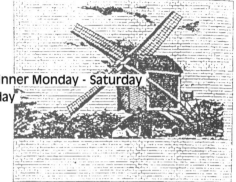

6807 West Becher
545-6970
West Allis
Breakfast, lunch and dinner Monday - Saturday
Breakfast only on Sunday
Smoking - yes
Bar - no
Bring cash
Dress: like a grandma

– home cooking –

The windows in Lynne's Kitchen have old-fashioned lace curtains, the kind that suggest an era when life moved to a slower beat. This cafe-coffee shop is a remnant of a small town restaurant frequented by another generation - a time when fast food meant Mom would fry a burger at home and serve it with canned corn and fried potatoes. There's a Norman Rockwell ambience at Lynne's. A nickel cup of coffee may be history, but regular customers keep a mug on the shelf and pay 15 cents for their bottomless cup. There's a shelf filled with homemade jam for sale. Who can resist pineapple-pear, raspberry, apricot, or apple butter?

They specialize in Broasted Chicken, that's chicken first marinated, then coated with a dry rub and deep fried to enhance the chicken's natural flavor. The result is a crisp, nutty golden-brown coating and juicy meat.

There's more to Lynne's than chicken. A sandwich and dessert make a splendid meal for less than $10, that includes a side order, a drink, and best of all, a slice of Lynne's homemade pie!

Ma Fischer's

2214 North Farwell
271-7424
Lower East Side
Breakfast, lunch and dinner every day
Smoking - yes
Bar - no
Bring cash
Dress: daytime, like a grandma; early evening, Bohemian; late
    evening, strange

EAT TASTY FOOD Special FARMER OMELETTE OPEN 24 HRS.

– the kitchen sink, predominately greek –

Whatever you can think of, whether day or night, there's a
good chance you'll find it on the menu at Ma Fischer's.
Ten pages plus a daily insert pretty well covers the universe of
cheap food. Its location, or the availability of parking in a
congested area, or senior specials, or all of the above, bring
crowds of customers to this former diner. Now expanded, it's
not small anymore. A brief stop on a Sunday around noon, and
the restaurant was so crowded families spilled out the front
door onto Farwell. Weekdays at the same time, it's jammin'
with senior citizens, and late at night it gets pretty, you know,
far out weird.

There was a Ma Fischer who retired in 1975. Today the owner
is George Panos, thus the Greek influence. The food is pretty
good, the restaurant is an institution near the Oriental Theater,
and if you're hungry for an oversized omelet, come for Ma
Fischer's and you won't leave hungry.

Maharaja

1550 North Farwell
276-2250
Lower East Side
Lunch and dinner every day
Smoking - yes
Wine and beer
MC, V, AE
Dress: something long, men wear a headdress

– indian –

Finally there's an Indian restaurant on the Lower East Side, where a large population of adventuresome diners, who are willing to try something they can't pronounce, are dining and loving what they're eating. Maharaja has not disappointed either Indian cuisine aficionados or customers who come to give the cuisine of a country halfway around the world a first try. As with other local Indian restaurants, they serve a lunch buffet, and for people unfamiliar with Indian food, it's a good first choice. Just remember the name of the dish you especially enjoyed, so you can find it again on the extensive dinner menu.

If it helps, a vindaloo is a curry, meat or seafood, cooked with potatoes and usually very warm spices. The menu gives fair warning for "hot" entrees. Just in case, order nam, bread baked in a tandoori oven or raita, a condiment made of cucumber and mint in yoghurt, served to remove some of the heat. If you've never tried lassi, order a Sweet Lassi, there's not a cooler drink on a hot day, or one that goes down better with Indian food. It's a simple yoghurt drink, flavored with rosewater and a sweetener.

Maria's Pizza

5025 West Forest Home
543-4606
Southwest Milwaukee
Dinner Tuesday - Sunday
Smoking - yes
Bar - no
Bring cash
Dress: don't wear red, you'll clash with the decor

- italian -

Walking into Maria's is like arriving at a festive family celebration. The dining room swirls with little blinking lights, glittering garlands, blow-up Easter bunnies, and religious paintings. Maria Memoralia is everywhere and so is the color red, from the ceiling to the waitress wearing a red suit and red platform heels. Tables are covered with red and white checked plastic cloth, some which has been repaired with transparent tape. By now you can guess this isn't a fancy joint. Soft drinks are served in paper cups and no one rushes to clear the table when the customers leave.

Pizza is the main meal here. The chef is known for the "amoeba" shaped crust, thin, tasty and clearly unique. It's hard to spend much money at Maria's if one orders pizza, as most do. The most pricey is the pepperoni supreme for $13 with cheese, sausage, mushrooms, onions, black olives, and green peppers. The garlic bread is good, but don't order the spaghetti, covered with watery sauce and canned mushrooms.

Mazo's

3146 South 27th Street
671-2118
South Side
Breakfast and lunch Monday - Friday
Open until 7:00 p.m. on Saturday
Smoking - no
Bar - no
Bring cash
Dress: comfortable

– good non-fancy cooking –

A sign on the wall reads "John Mazo's 1934, First Restaurant in Milwaukee, sold hamburgers for 5 cents." Three generations of Mazos later, they're still flipping burgers and serving them on toasted buns with more than a drop of butter. The homemade sausage on the breakfast menu is a Paul Bunyan-sized portion that covers half your plate. Underneath, they slip in home fries, again with extra butter, and two eggs done to order.

If you're a car buff, plan extra time for a leisurely visit. A gallery of auto trivia and related paraphernalia decorates each booth. They have a fascinating collection of antique license plates, old photos, framed newspaper articles, old Ford posters, and advertisements from magazines and newspapers. It's like a visit to the Art Museum, but it's free, and it's someone's personal collection.

McBob's Pub and Grill

4919 West North Avenue
871-5050
West Side
Lunch and dinner every day
Smoking - yes
Full bar
Bring cash
Dress: a kilt or perhaps a wee scotch plaid with jeans

– bar food –

Another gem - a neighborhood bar where the walls are covered with memoirs of the Scotch and Irish and the clientele is jolly. On Taco Days, Tuesday, Thursday and Saturday, customers line up for take-out and the pub rocks at lunchtime. Tacos in a Celtic bar? There's a legend to explain everything. Here it is:

"As the Celtic tribes traveled across Europe seeking their lands of freedom, they sojourned in what is now called Central Europe...We find that the now famed Taco actually has its genesis in the ancient usage of the work DOK-LO or the Old English word TAEGEL both meaning a plug or a nail." Hence McBob's serves the "beste soffte schelled Tacos in this citie." Sure!

They're good, really good, and cheap. McBob's, also known for burgers, serves a Mex Burger with hot peppers, and a Patti Melt with fried onions and Swiss on toasted rye. One can't spend more than $5 for a deluxe sandwich and fries. For health conscious customers, they'll grill a Ranch Turkey Burger with Swiss cheese. Even an 8-ounce New York Strip au jus, served on Monday, costs just $5. No wonder the *Shepard Express* readers voted McBob's "the best neighborhood bar" in 1996.

McGinn's

5901 West Bluemound Road
475-7546
Milwaukee West, close to Brewer stadium
Lunch and dinner every day
Brunch on Sunday
Smoking - yes
Full bar
MC, V, AE
Dress: baseball hat and jeans

– bar food –

It's a sports bar, but one with good food and enough side rooms where the TV won't be turned on, and one won't need ear plugs to converse across the table - unless you come on Packer Sunday when sports fans take over. However, McGinn's has a popular Sunday brunch featuring a farmer's omelet, a seafood omelet, a Mexican omelet or morning bun French toast, each served with fruit and coffee. For the frugal, on Monday from 5:00 p.m. to 10:00 p.m. the Blue Plate Special, tenderloin tips, mom's meatloaf, or turkey breast, each served with garlic mashed potatoes and garlic bread, will set you back a mere $4. Now those are depression-era prices.

Reviewer's favorite meals: tenderloin tips, Friday fish fry with homemade potato pancakes, and the Saturday special, 12 ounces of thick grilled pork chops.

Mel's Diner

3232 South 27th Street
389-9555
South Side
Breakfast, lunch and dinner every day
Smoking - yes
Full bar
MC, V
Dress: poodle skirt and bobby socks, Elvis hair for the guys

– 50's food –

Mel's, located on a busy street, stands out at first glance when one notices the front of a 1950s Chevy pasted on the wall facing 27th Street. If the lights are on, it's a good sign the restaurant's open. Enter the parking lot and see the rest of this vintage auto, with a 90s vanity plate that says what else? "Mel's." A sign proclaims, "Where Elvis is king and Chevys still rule." The door is just beyond the Texaco pump, a reminder of bygone times when all gas contained lead and cost 33 cents a gallon.

Non-smokers should ask for the non-smoking section; it's small but if you don't, you're likely to be seated where you don't want to be. 1950s bebop music sets the tone and toes tapping. Although larger than the usual diner, Mel's still has that special feeling some of us remember from those days. What could be more retro than Mel's Meatloaf, a Mel-waukee Must? They serve it on Texas toast with lettuce, tomato and onion. It takes a mighty big mouth to get around it, but I managed! This generous slab of meatloaf rated with Mom's, and served with chips - it's a meal for a mere $3.95. Breakfasts too are a reason to visit Mel's. A cheddar cheese omelet with rye toast and American fries will start your day on a sunny track.

Mercado El Rey

1023 South 16th Street
643-1640
South Side
Open every day
Smoking - yes
No booze
Bring cash
Dress: colorful

– mexican –

Yes - this is a grocery store. The restaurant's hidden behind the cases of soda and just beyond toiletries and household supplies. They dish up unpretentious Mexican food at reasonable prices. As you see in Mexico, a combination plate, covered with saran wrap, sits on the steam table so the uninitiated can see what's for dinner.

Front row seats at the counter make a good place to watch the grill show. First the grill person briefly sautés pre-cooked beef, chicken, pork or tongue for tacos, burritos, tostadas or chimichangas,while the corn or flour tortillas heat up on the grill. Then the sauté chef hands the tortilla and meat to the salad chef, who adds fresh reds and greens and drops it into a basket. Then a waiter/waitress gives it to a hungry diner, and finally a dishwasher washes and washes endless stacks of dishes. The system works. It's simple, efficient and impressive.

A $1.25 taco consists of two soft corn tortillas, choice of meat, lettuce, tomato, chopped parsley, and generous slices of avocado. Homemade red and green salsa is served in black bowls, alongside separate bowls of very hot peppers. Most customers drink orange or lemonade, made from real oranges, lemons, and limes squeezed on the premises. Almost everyone at El Rey speaks Spanish, and Mexican music plays on the speakers. For a quick deja vu visit to Mexico, stop in at Mercado El Rey.

MiKelly's

7225 West North Avenue
475-1315
Breakfast and lunch every day
Smoking - yes in a specific area
Bar - no
Bring cash
Dress: optional

– neighborhood cafe food –

Neighborhood restaurants are sprouting and blooming in Milwaukee. People love going to a place where someone calls them by name, especially if the name-caller is one of the owners. MiKelly's is that kind of place. Even the name is folksy, a combination of the owner's names, Mike and Shelly.

They have a passion for breakfast pecans, and the rumor mill says, "don't miss the Banana-Pecan Pancakes." Not to belabor the point, but the bananas and pecans are baked inside the batter, not spooned on top, yet the pancake is light and fluffy. Speaking of pecans, they also serve fried, sliced pecan-cinnamon loaf. One can't spend more than $7.95 for breakfast, and that's for steak and eggs. The Banana Pancakes, served with four slices of bacon plus coffee will set you back less than $6.

For lunch, burgers and sandwiches are on the menu, and for calorie counters, "Calorie Clipper" dishes include fruit, cottage cheese, and tuna or egg salad.

MiKelly's is small with counter seating for six and a dozen tables and booths. Since they're open until 7:00 p.m. on Fridays, of course there's a fish fry.

Mike's Red Hots

6914 North Teutonia Avenue
228-7080
Lunch and dinner Monday - Saturday
Come early, they close at 6:00 p.m. and 5:00 p.m. on Saturday
Smoking - no
No booze
Bring cash
Dress: anything goes

– carryout only — hotdogs of course –

There are hundreds of these places in Chicago, and fewer than five in Milwaukee. We have beer bars and brats, they have Vienna Hot Dogs. Why are they called "Chicago-Style Hot Dogs? Probably because they're made in Chicago. Chicago Style with the Works means mustard, relish, onions, tomato, pickle, pepper, and a steamed dog on a steamed poppy seed bun.

Since the early 80s, Mike has added nachos, fish, subs, chicken, and Italian meatball sandwiches to the menu, but the reason to seek out Mike's has always been the real thing. Take extra napkins, let the juice run down your chin and indulge in an all-American tradition that's here to stay.

Milwaukee Ale House

233 North Water Street
226-BEER
Third Ward
Lunch and dinner Monday - Saturday
Bar open on Sunday, but not the kitchen
Smoking - yes (only in the bar)
Full bar
MC, V, AE
Dress: thirty-something stylish

– upscale bar food –

The dinner menu doesn't make the $10 cut, but do visit this trendy 3rd Ward bar/restaurant and order from the soup and sandwich menu instead. A bowl of Water Street Gumbo made with chicken and Andouille sausage and a pub burger is more than enough for a meal. Wash it down with one of their six homemade brews. After all, this is a microbrewery. If you can't decide, try the sampler, a small glass of each of their house brews.

The Ale House is located at the confluence of the Milwaukee and Menomonee Rivers in a building known as the Saddlery Building, first built in 1868. Three times ravaged by fire, it was reconstructed last in 1894 using Cream City brick.

The brick, as well as the exposed rafters and heating vents give a historic ambience, and cloth napkins and oriental rugs showcased on hardwood floors add a classy touch. Since opening in October 1997, the Ale House has enjoyed an enthusiastic clientele. When the double decker beer garden opens, one might expect to see well-deserved standing room only.

Miss Katie's Diner

1900 West Clybourn
344-0044
Downtown
Breakfast, lunch and dinner every day
Smoking - yes (a few non-smoking tables in the front of the
    restaurant)
Full bar
MC, V, AE
Dress: Monday to Friday - power suits, weekend - jeans

– american –

M iss Katie's started out to be Milwaukee's version of
Chicago's Ed Debrevic's. For the period look, they hung
Allan Teger and Edward Hopper posters on the walls. Chrome
chairs and black Formica tabletops belong to the "I Love Lucy"
era, and speckled green and black floors appropriately match
the tables and chairs, just like the green and black kitchens of
the 1950s. Today the place looks more like the 90s, and diners
don't get front row seats anymore to watch the grill chef pour
grease on the potatoes. But, the kitchen still turns out blue-
plate specials and people still come for Miss Katie's homemade
meatloaf, oven-roasted turkey and roast sirloin of beef. Of
course they're all served with lots of mashed potatoes and
gravy. The same people who own Pitch's own Miss Katie's, so
barbecued ribs share the spotlight with the 50s food.

Miss Katie's claim to fame is the 1997 presidential visit when
President Clinton came to dine with Germany's Helmut Kohl.
A luncheon to remember!!!

Moy Fa Cafe

6119 West North Avenue
258-9800
Wauwatosa
Lunch, Monday - Saturday
Dinner every day
Smoking - no
Beer and wine
MC, V
Dress: up or down

– chinese –

The Moy Fa Cafe has become an institution on North Avenue. After twenty years, they've captured a piece of the West Side market for their homestyle Chinese food. Moy Fa translates as Plum Blossom, and to the family means the "blossoming of a culinary experience which blends the best from traditional Chinese cooking for today's demanding lifestyles."

As in most Chinese restaurants, the menu is extensive, with prices from $5.15 for Vegetable Egg Foo Yung (three patties served with rice) to $9.95 for Lobster Kow or Lobster Cantonese. Reviewers found the Egg Foo Yung especially tasty, but the Sweet and Sour Shrimp tasted reheated, and they didn't care for the lukewarm tea. Cloth napkins add a touch of class, but bare Formica tables need a cloth covering to upgrade from minimal to cozy. Could that be the reason their carryout business exceeds their sit-down trade?

Mr. Perkins

2001 West Atkinson
447-6660
Milwaukee
Breakfast, lunch and dinner Monday - Saturday
Smoking - yes
Bar - no
Bring cash
Dress: nicely

– real southern cooking –

For 30 years Mr. Perkins has been a Milwaukee tradition. You won't find a friendlier restaurant in this book! Everyone's talking, smiling, laughing, while feasting on huge portions of down home southern cooking. The original Mr. Perkins (Will Perkins, Sr.) will most likely greet you, and at once you feel at home. The service is excellent, everything is cooked to order, and you can't imagine a better piece of coconut pie. Everyone seems to know everyone else, yet a stranger will feel at ease and can easily join in the inter-table banter. When they ran out of maple syrup at a table adjacent to mine, the waitress came right back with a quart-size container. They take good care of their customers.

One can order grits, stewed apples, fried green tomatoes, turnip greens, black-eyed peas, oxtails or chitterlings. An ordinary breakfast of scrambled eggs, country bacon, homemade buttery biscuits and home fried potatoes is a delight, served with orange juice and plenty of good strong coffee. It's a popular stop for the pols when elections are coming up, and according to the insiders' grapevine, even the mayor comes here once in a while.

North Shore Bistro

River Point Shopping Center (Brown Deer Road and Port
    Washington Road)
8649 North Port Washington Road
351-6100
Fox Point
Lunch and dinner every day
Smoking - only in the bar
Full bar
MC, V, AE
Dress: upscale chic

– fancy food at reasonable prices –

Italians call a small, unpretentious restaurant a trattoria. The French refer to the same as a bistro. Milwaukee's North Shore Bistro comes across as cozy and unpretentious. The meals are reasonably priced, the staff is attentive, and one will find an eclectic mix of diners dressed in suits, silk, or jeans.

This was one of the first local restaurants to give beepers to the waitstaff to ensure your meal arrives as soon as it is ready in the kitchen. It's a high-tech operation where the waitperson enters each order into a computer that transmits it to the kitchen, and when the food is ready, your waitperson's beeper "beeps."

Everything is good here. Salads are lightly dressed according to today's tastes, the bread is fresh and warm, the flavors are subtle and the Chicken Pot Pie is fantastic. Don't miss the Gorgonzola Pasta, with artichokes, toasted walnuts, Roma tomatoes and Gorgonzola cheese served over spinach fettuccini.

Oakland Gyros

2867 North Oakland
963-1393
Shorewood
Open every day for lunch and dinner (close 3:00 a.m.)
Smoking - yes
Bar - no
Bring cash
Dress: a Greek fisherman's hat and Doc Martens

– greek, especially gyros –

This is one of the many corner restaurants I've passed hundreds of times. I knew if I ever craved a gyros, this was the place, so on a Sunday about 1:00 p.m. I dropped in to check out their best-known menu item. I should have brought a friend. A gyros here isn't just a sandwich, it's a meal. It's also not really a sandwich. Underneath multiple layers of tender meat, sliced onions, tomatoes and sauce, there's a pita hiding.

This is a great place for Greek food that's cheap. The spinach pie at an adjacent table looked big enough for two and so did the salad. Since it's fast food-style, order at the counter and then stay as long as you wish. No one will rush you, even if they're busy. The cooks are Greek, the music Greek, portions gargantuan, and the view out the windows looking at Oakland, never dull.

In addition to the gyros, other specialties include beef or chicken shishkabob, rice pilaf, spinach pie, moussaka, Athenian chicken, lamb shank and Greek salad. For the less adventuresome, the chef will cook a burger, an all-beef hot dog, or a fish sandwich. Unlike most fast food places, when I got up to leave, a person came at once to clear my tray before I could take care of it myself. Could that be the reason Oakland Gyros is immaculate?

Oakland Trattoria

2856 North Oakland Avenue
964-2850
Lower East Side
Lunch and dinner every day
Smoking - no
Bar - yes
MC, V, AE
Dress: rustic jeans

– country italian –

At Oakland Trattoria, the emphasis, according to our charming waitperson is on "food you would eat at your grandma's house." He meant good, simply prepared Italian home cooking, done on a wood fire, and priced so families can afford the tab.

People who remember the old German Kalt's, formerly at this location, won't recognize this new layout. It's spacious and divided into four separate rooms, including a back room with a fireplace available to groups. The menu varies from wood fired pizza, to a variety of salads, to pasta with tomato or marinara sauce, to a few chicken dishes, sandwiches, a Friday fish fry, and for dessert, tiramisu. I found the Wood Roasted Vegetable Salad especially delicious. They roast eggplant, zucchini, peppers, green beans and red potatoes, mix them with greens and toss the salad with a rosemary-balsamic dressing that's euphoric. I could eat it every day.

The Chicken Picata is good, served with pasta and roast vegetables, the freshly baked focaccia is delicious, especially when dipped in olive oil. At dinnertime bring earplugs and be prepared to wait. Service is very slow.

The Trattoria is owned by the same people who own Turner Hall, thus the Friday fish fry is identical to the one downtown, and if you've experienced a Turner Hall fish fry, you know it's good.

Oriental Coast

1230 East Brady Street
278-8680
Lower East Side
Lunch and dinner every day except Sunday
Dinner only on Sunday
Smoking - yes
Full bar
MC, V
Dress: casual

– chinese-cantonese –

This isn't your typical Chinese restaurant. It's upbeat and upscale with shiny black chairs, white cloths on the tables and New Age music to remind you that these are the 90s. Owner Allen Tsao came to Milwaukee from Shanghai via Marquette University, where he earned a master's degree in molecular biology. But he always loved to cook, and he opened Oriental Coast in 1993 with his father and his uncle.

Unlike many Chinese restaurants, they don't use MSG in the food unless a purchased sauce will have it as one of the ingredients.

Vegetarian Egg Rolls are a favorite as are Pot Stickers, steamed to perfection. The latter must be taken in a single bite as the Chinese do, otherwise the juicy center will be lost. Hot and Sour Soup is delicious, and so is everything else on the menu. Of note is Lo Mein, hot enough to remind you of cayenne, but not too hot to enjoy every bite and still have enough for another meal at home. If you're lucky, they'll have some Chinese broccoli in the kitchen and at a customer's request, will prepare this special dish.

Outpost Natural Foods

100 East Capitol Drive
961-2597
Just east of I-43
Open 7 days a week (hours vary)
Smoking - no
No booze
MC, V, AE, checks ok
Dress: for shopping

– grocery store-deli –

The Outpost started in the 1960s with a neighborhood group that formed a buying co-op. When their operation outgrew their storage capacity, the next step was a Locust Street storefront. From Locust, they quadrupled their space at Keefe and Holton, and two years ago moved into their present location.

Over the years, Outpost has evolved from a place to shop for dry fruit, beans, grains, nuts, and seeds to a full service grocery store, where today they stock the largest selection of natural foods and organic produce in Wisconsin.

The food service here comes from the deli, where they offer a variety of delicious soups and sandwiches. They'll sell you hot sandwiches, burritos, bagels from Madison Bagel Company, bakery from La Boulangerie, apple, pumpkin and blueberry bars from Livin Bread Bakery, and their own home-made cookies and carrot cake. They offer a soup of the day such as African Bean or Southern Indian Lentil, and a variety of salads like Pineapple Bulgur, Spinach-Chick Pea-Feta, Mediterranean Lentil, Tabouli, or Wild Rice.

To keep up on new restaurant openings as well as on golden oldies, read my reviews in the *Outpost Exchange*, a free monthly publication available at many locations, including the Outpost.

Palermo Villa

2315 North Murray Avenue
278-7460
Lower East Side
Dinner every day
Smoking - in the bar area
Full bar
MC, V, AE
Dress: jeans are fine, add jewels or a blazer on Saturday night

- italian -

Back in the 70s, Palermo was a typical Italian bistro with red checked tablecloths in a dark interior, and colored candles dripping over green Chianti bottles. They served multi-course meals, and although the food was always good, it was just too much for today's lighter appetites.

After a fire in 1981, owner Kathleen Mirenda decided a more contemporary look suited both her clientele and the new menu, so she painted the walls peach, installed track lights to show off her poster collection and added a mirrored wall to visually expand the space. Now it looks like the sort of restaurant some of us can't afford to visit in Florence or Venice.

The waitstaff won't rush you, and it's a good place to relax with a glass of red wine and a basket of Italian bread while you think about the menu. They offer unusual pizzas and one of the best, probably because it oozes with fat calories, is White Pizza Neapolitan.

In addition to pizza, Palermo offers a wide selection of appetizers, including French fried eggplant, appetizer breads, seafood a la carte, many different pasta dinners, and mouth watering Italian selections such as spedini, lightly breaded beef tenderloin stuffed with cheese and baked.

Park View Restaurant

821 West Lincoln Avenue
649-8080
South Side
Breakfast, lunch and dinner every day
Smoking - yes
Bar - no
Bring cash
Dress: overalls

– diner food –

A serendipitous find happened when I was working on another book and landed hot and thirsty at the corner of 8th and Lincoln. I wandered into this unassuming little restaurant, ordered a chicken breast sandwich in a basket and a cup of homemade soup du jour and ended up with a feast. I've returned many times to sample the turkey club, the good greasy cheeseburger and the regular burger smothered with fried onions. Leave calorie counters behind and enjoy an old-fashioned neighborhood place where everyone else seems to know each other.

Park View has been here for eighteen years but it feels more like a diner that came to this South Side neighborhood with the original settlers. Nearby are two favorite stops for me, Lincoln Avenue Pottery at 66th and Lincoln, and Lopez Bakery on the southwest corner of Lincoln and 16th Streets.

The Pasta Tree

1503 North Farwell
276-8867
Lower East Side
Dinner every night
Smoking - no
Wine and beer
MC, V
Dress: Lower East Side chic

– italian –

Yes, it's crowded but that's part of the charm in this bistro that fills up seven nights a week. The Pasta Tree's talented and friendly waitstaff deserve applause as they weave in and around diners seated in two narrow rows.

Don't show up here if you count fat grams with every bite. On the other hand, if you lust after homemade bread with real butter, pasta in a rich cream sauce, and lush homemade desserts, you've just found nirvana.

Pasta courses range from Tomato-Meat Sauce, to Scallops and Artichokes in Cream, to Shrimp Broccoli, to specialty pastas such as cheese-stuffed manicotti or tortellini. Pasta Pigliara has shrimp, scallops, mussels and salmon in an olive herb sauce. A delicious salad precedes the main course.

Intrepid diners should remember to save room for dessert. Grand Marnier Cheesecake, Flourless Chocolate Cake, Chocolate Chip Cookies, and much more rotate each week.

Pavillion

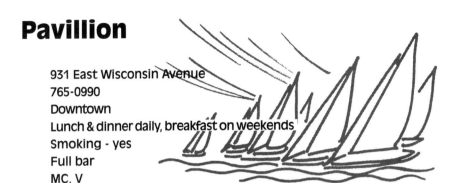

931 East Wisconsin Avenue
765-0990
Downtown
Lunch & dinner daily, breakfast on weekends
Smoking - yes
Full bar
MC, V
Dress: jeans to Brooks Brothers with stylish suits and silk ties

– you name it –

Isn't life strange? We live in a "great city on a great lake" yet we lack restaurants that take advantage of the magnificent view available to anyone who walks alongside Lake Michigan, or admires the harbor from atop a bluff. Finally, as of 1996, there's a notable exception to this scarcity, the Pavillion, a moderately priced restaurant at the end of Wisconsin Avenue by the di Suvero sculpture. Not only does the restaurant offer lovely views of the harbor, it offers a patio to accommodate dozens of diners who prefer the lake breeze, fresh air and on occasion, sunshine.

An extensive menu includes Greek, Mexican, Indian and Italian dishes as well as omelets, sandwiches, salads and burgers. Spinach pie, $6.95, makes a delicious lunch or dinner and comes with rice, vegetable, chicken soup with dumplings the way grandma made them, and dessert, a choice between bread or rice pudding. The spinach pie, filo dough layered with fresh spinach and a generous amount of feta cheese, makes a superb entrée and one with value that far exceeds its reasonable price.

Pedrano's

600 South 6th Street
276-6880
Walker's Point
11:00 a.m. - 10:00 p.m. every day
Smoking - yes
Bar - yes
MC, V
Dress: jeans, sombrero optional

– mexican –

This is another story of a family's determination to pull together and make a miracle. It began when the Castillo family opened their Mexican restaurant on 6th Street in 1991. It was quickly recognized as a place where one could expect authentic Mexican food at good prices. Since the family had been in the catering business for many years, operating from their home in West Bend, they had established a reputation for good food prior to opening Pedrano's.

In 1995, fire destroyed the restaurant and almost snuffed out the dream, but the family didn't give up and reopened the same year. Gloria Castillo runs the kitchen and does the cooking using recipes she brought to Milwaukee from her village when she immigrated to Milwaukee in 1966. There are many family-run restaurants to choose from in Walker's Point - this is one of the best.

Pier 221

221 Water Street
283-9244
Third Ward
Breakfast and lunch Wednesday - Sunday
Smoking - no
Bar - no
Bring cash
Dress: funky

– soup, sandwiches and salads –

Pier 221 is hiding behind an art gallery that used to be a lighting store on Water Street. It's a charming, bright room, adjacent to the Milwaukee River. Orange and blue walls, one cream city brick wall, and unusual lighting fixtures create a welcoming space for breakfast or lunch. There's an interesting collection of art on the walls and comfortable deck chairs to sit in while gazing at the action on the river or the trains roaring past just across the water. Faraway, toy cars move slowly across the Hoan Bridge. There you are, enjoying lunchtime entertainment that includes cars, trains, busses, trucks and boats.

The food is OK. I found my burrito unfortunately swimming in something that suspiciously resembled melted Cheez Whiz™, but my friend said her unlimited soup and salad combo was delicious.

Pikmar Restaurant

7276 North Teutonia Avenue
352-4650
Northwest Side
Breakfast and lunch every day
Smoking - yes
No booze
Bring cash
Dress: a bowling shirt with your jeans

– 50s diner food –

Word of mouth led me to this working-class restaurant on Milwaukee's Northwest Side where a suit and tie would be out of place. At a late breakfast, the restaurant was crowded with retirees, mostly male, and buzzed with an undercurrent of conversation. It's a great choice for people who want home cooking away from home, but have to work within a meager budget.

Owner Lisa Lipski posts daily specials on a board behind the counter, and $4 buys potatoes, roll, salad, and the special meat dish. She has fifty specials and offers them in a five-week rotation.

At lunch, a soup and sandwich special for $3 includes split pea soup with a liver sausage sandwich, or homemade vegetable soup with an egg salad sandwich. Could this be the 50s again? The name, Pikmar, sounds more like a dental supply business than a restaurant. The name came about when the original owners combined their names, and it's stuck for thirty years.

Pitch's

1801 North Humboldt
272-9313
Brady Street neighborhood
Lunch and dinner Monday - Friday
Dinner Saturday and Sunday
Smoking - yes
Full bar
MC, V, AE
Dress: whatever, but try to arrive in a large black car

– bar food and ribs –

This long-established Lower East Side restaurant has earned a well-deserved reputation for Bar-B-Q ribs. People who consider themselves aficionados come from great distances to dine on ribs at this unpretentious corner restaurant. The rib sandwich is likewise tender and tasty with the same sauce, and served with hash browns, it makes a full meal. The potatoes also have earned a reputation as one of Milwaukee's finest potato side dishes. The chef boils, cools, peels, shreds, and fries each order in enough butter to let you know butter is a main ingredient.

Pitch's, a family endeavor, was founded in 1942 by John and Katherine Picciurro, parents of the current proprietor, Peter Picciurro Senior.

The service is good, the restaurant is seldom crowded, and it's recommended for lunch or dinner. Pitch's offers a taste of ribs along with a chance to rub elbows with members of Milwaukee's Italian Lower East Side community, enjoying a meal while their dogs bark and alarms in their black cars chime in the parking lot.

Pizza Man

1800 East North Avenue
272-1745
Lower East Side
Lunch Saturday and Sunday
Dinner every day
Smoking - yes
Full bar
MC, V, AE, checks ok
Dress: anything goes, it's dim and private

- italian -

Sometimes good food shows up in unexpected places. Pizza Man sounds more like fast food than solid Italian fare, and hardly a place to look for fine wine. In fact they have one of the best wine cellars in metro Milwaukee. They showcase their wine every other Tuesday at a reservation-only tasting that includes a dinner to enhance the pleasure of the grape.

Enter through a sturdy wooden door into an inviting bar and small restaurant with a couple of dozen tables and wooden booths. If you treat yourself to a glass of the daily house special wine, you'll know this isn't California "Gallo by the goblet." Ah, the pleasure of slow anticipation of escargot, garlic bread and "Hail Caesar Salad." The entrees are eclectic Italian, served with abundant heavy cream, sweet butter and fresh garlic. Pizza Man chefs cook Italian style, and they do it right. Lasagna, mostaccioli, fettucini, linguini, or tortellini; it's all good. So is the pizza; in fact, the thin crust variety with sausage, black olives, and onions rivals any pizza in Milwaukee.

High-backed wooden booths keep dinner for two a private affair, and soft classical music brings a genteel note to the atmosphere. Outside the back door, a tiny dining area bordered by a wood fence and Oakland Avenue adds romance and candlelight on a warm summer evening.

Polonez

4016 S. Packard (moving from 2316 S. 6th Street)
482-0080 (384-8766)
St. Francis
Lunch and dinner every day – a new Saturday buffet
    and Sunday brunch
Smoking - no
Beer, wine, a few mixed drinks
No credit, checks ok
Dress: nicely

– polish –

Polonez is scheduled to open at the Packard address in September 1999. There are many good reasons to visit Polonez, including a friendly cafe atmosphere where diners talk between tables, excellent Polish food, and owner Wladyslaw Burznski, known simply as George. He and his staff prepare great Polish food at reasonable prices, and George serves it with a big smile and a sense of humor. Be sure to ask him about the *Minneapolis Star and Tribune* restaurant review dated February 28, 1993. He doesn't know how, but there's Polonez listed as one of Milwaukee's finest restaurants along with Boders, Maders, and Jack and George Pandl's. Not bad for a factory worker turned restauranteur who came to the United States to live in a democratic country. George and his wife opened Polonez in 1983 and they worked hard. They still do. Back then she held an office job and during her lunch hour, waited on tables at the restaurant.

For a first visit and a sampling of regional food, Polski Talerz is highly recommended. The plate includes a large stuffed cabbage roll, Polish sausage, sauerkraut, a boiled potato and three pierogi, one stuffed with sauerkraut, one stuffed with meat, and one stuffed with a lightly sweetened cheese filling. They make soup daily, and mushroom, barley, and borsch are all best sellers. They also offer American food, but why go to an ethnic restaurant to order a burger?

Pomodoro's

7335 Greenfield Avenue
778-1990
West Allis
Lunch and dinner Tuesday - Sunday
Smoking - small area for smokers
Bar - wine only at the time of publication
MC
Dress: no bikinis, air conditioning works too well

– italian –

Pomodoro is not the family name of the owners, it's Italian for tomato as in Roma, the tomato the Italians prefer to use in cooking. This is a family restaurant, a newcomer, operated by Julie and Gino Zeneli, a couple who are not newcomers to the restaurant business. They offer Italian cuisine at neighborhood prices. This way, whole families can enjoy dinner out, instead of just Mom and Dad while the kids stay at home with a babysitter.

It's hard to believe dinners start at $6.95 and include soup or salad and garlic bread. The only double-digit dinner entree is Mixed Seafood, Shrimp, Clams and Mussels, in a Red Marinara over Linguini, $10.95.

The Eggplant Parmesan is outstanding, as is the Veal Marsala with fresh mushrooms and a marsala wine sauce with just a touch of tomato. The homemade pasta dinners served *en casserole* are delicious and moderately priced, and the Chicken Parmigiana is fabulous. There's no reason to have the fish fry on Friday, as the chef's skill lies in turning out authentic Italian dishes.

Avoid the two booths on the wall closest to Greenfield Avenue, or you'll hear the dessert cooler compressor, otherwise the restaurant is quiet and conducive to conversation.

Q F & H Diner

3349 North Martin Luther King Drive
372-2710
Near North Side
Breakfast, lunch and early dinner every day
Smoking - yes
Bar - no
MC, V, AE
Dress: anything goes

– soul food –

This small restaurant, two booths, two tables, and a counter with five stools, has earned an impressive reputation for soul food in Milwaukee. In addition to serving meals at the diner on Martin Luther King Drive, they have an extensive catering business.

Q F & H started in 1961 when a restaurant space on Burleigh became available, and a neighbor, a jeweler, contacted Mrs. Josephine Hicks about opening a restaurant. The space was empty, and it was known she was interested in the food business. Soon Mrs. Hicks formed a partnership with her sister Mrs. Pearl Qualls. They named their dinette the Q & F Diner. The groceries they needed for the opening fit in two bags, and the menu was simple: hamburgers, fries, fried chicken, and a pork chop dinner. Later they added H for Hicks to the restaurant's name, and today are known as the Q F & H Diner.

Come here for southern soul specialties. Every day seven dinner choices are available, served with a choice of two side dishes and cornbread. Sides include turnip and collard greens, potato salad, red beans and rice, okra, black-eyed peas, and more, but remember to save room for dessert. Who can resist real southern treats such as peach cobbler, bread pudding, sweet potato pie and the "cake of the day"?

The Rainbow

6290 South Martin Road
679-0490
New Berlin
Breakfast, lunch and dinner Tuesday - Saturday
Breakfast and lunch on Sunday
Closed Monday
Smoking - yes
Beer only
Bring cash
Dress: something washable, sometimes the smoke gets dense

– family restaurant cuisine –

O ccasionally I'm clueless. How did I learn about the
Rainbow? Maybe a friend of a friend told me about this
small family neighborhood place. The menu varies daily, and
the chef posts it on a blackboard. There's also a printed menu,
but it's more fun to order from the board. The Friday fry
comes highly recommended - cod or haddock, baked or fried
but always huge portions. In Milwaukee, that's enough to bring
people back.

Red Rock Cafe

(Fathom Five Seafood Market and Restaurant)

4022 North Oakland
962-4545
Shorewood
Lunch and dinner Tuesday - Saturday
Smoking-no
Wine and beer
MC, V
Dress: beret and turtleneck

– fish –

Guess what they specialize in here? Since the market adjoins the restaurant, the presence of fish on ice suggests what's on the menu, although it's different every day. Now Milwaukeeans can boast about an epicurean eatery where a grilled tuna steak sandwich, marinated and charbroiled, and a glass of Stevenot Cabernet Sauvignon costs less than two fins. Starched white tablecloths and fine china set in a jazzy New Orleans café-style atmosphere suit the menu. Or is it the other way around? The decibel level exceeds cozy, and walk-through traffic precludes romance, but the first-rate food rates at least three Michelin stars.

They marry mussels to saffron in Billy-Bi Soup, and our reviewers noted, "neither the mussels nor the saffron was overpowering." The sous-chef knows how to smooth a sauce, and lemon on scallops is superb. Fish fries include beer battered cod, breaded lake perch and jumbo fried shrimp. Count on a generous half-pound of fish, crispy French fries and homemade coleslaw.

Restaurant Hama

333 West Brown Deer Road (east end of Audubon Court)
352-5051
Fox Point
Lunch and dinner Monday-Saturday
Closed Sunday
Smoking - no
Beer, wine, and sake
MC, V, AE
Dress: Talbot's country club casual

– japanese fusion –

I stretch the $10 limit at Restaurant Hama, and it can't include the tip, but this is such a fine place to dine on the North Shore that I want to tell my readers about it, even though the cost exceeds my $10 limit. It's elegant, and one wouldn't be comfortable here in jeans, for the clientele is North Shore and they do dress up. But the food is fantastic, and let's face it, this is as close as Milwaukee comes to a sushi restaurant, albeit pricey. You know it's unusual at first peek into the elegant space, defined by a lovely peach and gray floor, undulating cherrywood rectangles and squares on the ceiling, and randomly spaced origami cranes to remind us we're in a Japanese restaurant. Of course the "tap tap" of the sushi chef's knife whets one's appetite for what's to come.

Fried Calamari Salad with Cilantro Dressing, Calamari Marinara Montrachet, and Spanish Paella with Green Salad almost fit into the price limit of this book. But the star at Restaurant Hama is the North Shore, $38 for two, a multi-course meal of Sushi, Sashimi (raw fish without rice), Tempura, Gyoza (resembles a potsticker) and Chicken Teriyaki. This is adventuresome dining. Bon appetit, or as they say on the islands "gochiso ni" (go she zo nee)!!!

Reynold's Pasty Shop

3525 West Burleigh Street
444-4490
West Side
9:00 a.m. - 6:30 p.m. Tuesday - Saturday
Bring cash
Dress: whatever

– carryout pasties –

It's not a pastry, it's a pasty, and it rhymes with fast, not taste. Occasionally someone wanders in from the street looking for doughnuts or apple pie, but that's not what they sell at Reynold's. Instead, they bake ground beef, chopped potato, onion and shredded carrots in a thin pastry crust and call it "a meal in itself." It is!

Traditionally, iron and copper miners in the Upper Peninsula carried a warm pasty into the mines for lunch. It's sort of a homemade transportable "fast food," only the franchise market hasn't discovered it. In lieu of a "drive through," the street parking's easy on Burleigh and the service quick. They'll sell you a warm pasty in a brown paper bag or one partially cooked, ready for the freezer, and another time. You can buy it with gravy or melted cheese, but the best way to eat a pasty is to load it with catsup. Reviewers comment, "ate pasties for years at Syl's in Ontonogan in the Upper Peninsula, and this one's better." For dessert, try the pecan pie by the slice or an apple turnover.

Rey Sol

2338 West Forest Home Avenue
389-1760
Southwest Side
Lunch and dinner every day
Smoking - yes
Bar - yes
MC, V
Dress: nicely

– mexican –

J ust home from three weeks in Mexico, a friend gave me an article about Rey Sol. I dined there the next night. Mexican food is so much more than Tex-Mex tacos and burritos, and here some of the best of the cuisine is on the menu. There's more than a hint of good things to come when a tray of appetizers is presented instead of chips and salsa. We each enjoyed a mini tostada de cerviche, two empanadas and a gordita, made with fresh corn dough. Each was delicious.

Jose "Pepe" Mendieta, owner and chef, greeted us and at our request for his favorite, suggested Beef Argentino. A few minutes later our waitress came to take the order and when we told her we weren't quite ready she reminded us of the Beef Argentino discussion, because he'd already put it on the grill. Good thing I ordered it, because this horizontal slice of fillet was fork tender and one of the best pieces of beef I've ever enjoyed. Served with rice, beans and corn tortillas, it was a delight. My companion ordered the Cochinita Pibil, Yucatan-style shredded pork with red onions and this too was a treat, unlike Tex-Mex and decidedly better. Pina Asada al Carbon con Licor Cacoa, or grilled pineapple with cacoa liquor, was an ideal finale to a fabulous dinner at Rey Sol.

Ricardo's

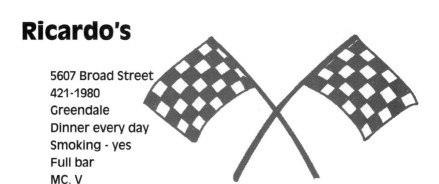

5607 Broad Street
421-1980
Greendale
Dinner every day
Smoking - yes
Full bar
MC, V
Dress: come in costume if you wish, anything goes

– primarily pizza –

What better recommendation is there for a restaurant than the regular attendance of other local restaurant owners? Ricardo's is Greendale's neighborhood watering hole, where locals gather any night of the week; the television promise "a place where everyone knows your name" is operative here. Ricardo's, owned by the Loch family, is the place to come if you want to talk auto racing. Memorial Day and Labor Day weekends, they book a bus to take fans to the Slinger Speedway where Rich Loch, the kitchen manager races the Ricardo's #55 car, and as they tell me, "a good time is had by all."

Ricardo's specialty is pizza, and they create some of the most innovative combos in town. For example, the BLT, cheese, bacon, fresh tomatoes topped with lettuce and mayo is a winner. Reviewers favorites include Eat Your Spinach, self-explanatory, and the Hawaiian, cheese, pineapple, and Canadian bacon. On the sandwich menu they have the Hummer, "don't ask," and an Italian sausage patty with sauce, onions, green pepper, and melted mozzarella. All sandwiches are served with fries and coleslaw. Prices range from $5 for a Naked Hummer to $5.75 for Chicken Mozzarella.

Rivers Edge Restaurant and Truck Stop

281 South Riverside Drive (just west of I-43 in Saukville)
284-9918
Saukville
Breakfast and lunch every day
Dinner until 8:00 p.m. Friday
Smoking - definitely
Bar - no
Bring cash
Dress: long haul driver garb if you sit at the counter

– diner food –

Ask me where I want to go for breakfast and I'll answer, "Rivers Edge!" I make the trip from Milwaukee to this Saukville truck stop often, and should have a standing order on file for breakfast. Scrambled eggs, home fries with fried onions, bacon, and homemade toast sound ordinary, but while you may consider the eggs ordinary, everything else is worth the drive. The potatoes are good and greasy, fried with lots of sweet onions; the bacon is thick, and I mean thick, fried ahead of time and then briefly deep fried just before serving; and the bread is homemade, sliced good and thick, served with butter and jam. It's hard to spend more than $6, and that includes coffee and a tip.

They make a variety of sandwiches, homemade soup, chili, dinners such as fried chicken, pork chops, and ham, plus haddock, perch, and shrimp seafood dinners. Polish this off with a wedge of homemade pie and you know you've had a trucker's meal, meant to last awhile.

Because truckers sit at the counter and many of them smoke, you will find it hard to escape the bad air, but nothing is perfect and the food here is worth the inconvenience of the smoking. I don't expect management to ban it soon, if ever.

Royal India Restaurant

3400 South 27th Street (across from Southgate
    Shopping Mall)
647-2050
South Side
Lunch and dinner every day
Smoking - no
Bar - no
MC, V, AE
Dress: sari optional

– indian –

Five years ago when I wrote *Milwaukee Eats,* there were no Indian restaurants in Milwaukee. In 1999 we have several, and according to "the media," Royal India rates A+. In a recent *Shepard Express* poll, it was named the best Indian restaurant in the city. Perhaps their readers had visited the $6.95 lunch buffet, one of the best values in town.

Most days the buffet will include two meat dishes, two vegetable dishes, two rice dishes, condiments, salad, dessert and naam, the traditional white flour bread baked in a tandoori (clay) oven. A typical buffet would include Vegetable Biryani, rice cooked with vegetables and nuts; Daal Makhni, lentils, spiced and cooked in butter; Onion Bhaji, crispy deep fried onions; Aloo Gobhi, cauliflower and potato cooked with tomato and onion; Mutter Paneer, green peas cooked in a mildly spiced gravy; Chicken Curry; and Lamb Vindaloo, lamb and potatoes cooked in a spicy gravy.

There's no better drink with this food than Lassi, made with homemade yoghurt flavored with rosewater. Is your mouth watering yet?

Rudy's

631 South 5th Street
291-0296
Walker's Point
Lunch and dinner every day
Smoking - yes
Full bar
MC, V, AE
Dress: suits at lunch and jeans at dinner

– mexican –

Rudy's has turned out to be one of Milwaukee's most popular South Side Mexican restaurants. Good easy parking on 5th Street brings in the lunch business crowd, and good food helps too. In an area saturated with tamales, tostados and tacos, they serve consistently good food at bargain prices. The restaurant is clean and tastefully decorated in typical southwestern Tex-Mex style.

Their popular combo plates called Laredo, Acapulco, or Rudy's Special, bring in regulars who feed on tacos, enchiladas, chimichangas and tostadas in a variety of combinations, each accompanied by rice and beans. Tamales are especially recommended, as are the chili rellenos.

Reviewers found the beef fajitas especially delicious, and decided Rudy's was a good choice for people who aren't used to coming south of downtown for ethnic food.

Sabor Latino

815 South 5th
384-6356
Walker's Point
Lunch and dinner every day
Smoking - yes
Full bar
MC, V, AE
Dress: comfy

– puerto rican –

They serve breakfast anytime at Sabor, numbers 23, 24, and 25 on the Mexican third of the menu. The rest of the Mexican menu lists the usual Tex-Mex flautas, tacos, enchiladas and so on. The American favorites, another third of the menu, lists burgers and fries, but the reason to visit Sabor Latino is the middle third, where the Puerto Rican specialties are found.

Moe Fontanez and his wife/partner Diana serve wonderful regional dishes and add a touch of Latino jazz with the Luis Diaz Quintet on Friday nights. Starting with appetizers, one can order the house favorite, Tostones, bananas lightly seasoned and deep-fried to golden brown. Reviewers also liked the slow-roasted pork, Pernil, served with rice, beans, salad, and bread; and also Bistec Encebollado, strips of beef covered with sweet sautéed onion. Other mouth-watering combinations include Pastel, the equivalent of a tamale with Puerto Rican vegetables and pork; and Sandwich de Pernil, a roast pork sandwich with sour cream, avocado, lettuce, and tomato. One can also buy this roast pork by the pound for an at-home Torta. With prices in the $6 - $7 range, fine quality and generous portions, Sabor in Walker's Point will be around for a while.

Saigon Restaurant

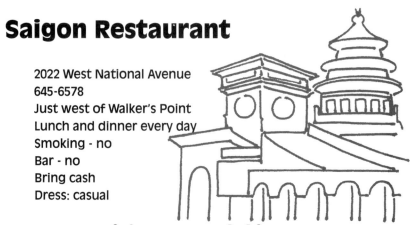

2022 West National Avenue
645-6578
Just west of Walker's Point
Lunch and dinner every day
Smoking - no
Bar - no
Bring cash
Dress: casual

– vietnamese and chinese –

The reason to come to Saigon isn't to try the Chinese dishes, which are tasty, but not nearly as unusual as the Vietnamese specialties. The Kung Po Delight, a Chinese dish is very good, filled with shrimp, beef, and chicken and topped with peanuts. A red-hot sauce on the table, one of several, adds the extra punch this dish needs. But the Pho Dac Biet Saigon, served in an oversized soup bowl, is fantastic. A side of lovely fresh greens accompanies the hot soup. The diner adds the greens to the soup, which partially cooks them before they're eaten as part of the dish. The fresh taste of the varied greens combined with the complicated flavors of the Pho is spectacular, and it took a member of my party back to her travels in Vietnam. If she had a complaint, it was that the greens cooled the soup. If one is served this dish in Vietnam, the soup comes on a burner, which keeps it hot while the greens are added, but here in Milwaukee individual burners wouldn't be up to code. For the real thing, you'll need to book a flight to Vietnam.

Saigon is a neighborhood restaurant that serves the local Vietnamese population as well as adventuresome diners from the greater Milwaukee area. The food is authentic, unadorned and delicious, and the restaurant is not fancy, but one where real food is served at budget prices.

Samano's Hacienda

3431 East Plankington Avenue
481-3664
Cudahy
Lunch Tuesday - Saturday
Dinner Tuesday - Sunday
Smoking - yes
Full bar
MC, V, Discover, checks ok
Dress: no one will notice

– mexican –

There's authentic Mexican food south of Milwaukee in one of the 'burbs. Samano's in Cudahy isn't fancy, but then what Mexican restaurant is? This family run corner restaurant has been turning out some of the tastiest basic Mexican meals in greater Milwaukee since the 60s.

The best way to sample their entrees is to taste as much as you can and still zip your jeans. Take a friend or two and a hearty appetite, and start with the appetizer sampler. This way you'll avoid making a choice between cheese and onion quesadillas, guacamole, bean dip, and nachos and chips. In the entree column, try the "original combination" that includes a beef taco, an enchilada, chili verde, rice, beans, and flour or corn tortillas. The corn tortilla can barely contain the meaty contents of the taco, the cheese enchilada oozes cheese, and the chili verde is rich with tender beef. The chimichanga dinner is a winner too, and for dessert, the bunuelos top the meal with a honey/sugar high. The bar serves nine different Mexican beers, a nice change from Corona or lite Corona, and Hacker-Pschorr on tap. If you run a neighborhood restaurant, you do it right or you're history, and after twenty-plus years the Samanos are still putting out fat tacos for the locals.

Saz's

5539 West State Street
453-2410
West Side
Lunch and dinner every day
Smoking - yes
Full bar
MC, V
Dress: baseball caps and sweats (ties permitted)

– pub food –

This "old Milwaukee" bar/restaurant tucked underneath the Hawley Street overpass draws crowds daily. Plan to wait for a table on Friday, but it's easy to pass time in the bar with a weiss beer and some munchies. Once seated, the service is fast and friendly, and modest prices bring locals again and again for food that is always worth the wait. You can't spend more than $21 for a New York Strip Steak, but you don't need to drop that much cash when you can get a rib sandwich with homemade chips or sour cream fries for $5. The meat overflows the bun, and there's no delicate way to eat the thing, so lick your fingers, wear a napkin bib, and enjoy! If you're there when the train rambles by, the vibrations will take you back to a sense of bygone times, and the good old days when everyone traveled by rail.

Saz's is busy when the Brewers are in town, and fans ride free to the games. Check out the bathrooms, they look more like a high school locker room latrine than a saloon restroom, but many commodes get riders to the games on time. If you have time, try the Caramel Apple Granny Cheesecake.

Seidita's Italian Deli and Catering

2921 North Oakland Avenue
962-1183
Lower East Side
Breakfast and lunch Monday - Saturday
Smoking - no
Bar - no
MC, V
Dress: red, white and green

– italian, eat-in or carry-out –

Until five years ago, Seidita's was a landmark meat market on the Lower East Side. There, one would always catch a whiff of fresh herbs as a butcher worked in the back of the store, stuffing their many sausage varieties. The good aroma remains, but in place of a meat market, there is an Italian deli.

They make a dozen sandwiches, both hot and cold; the best seller is Tony's Special, Italian sausage with green peppers, onions, and sauce. The sausage is made somewhere else, but the recipe is the same one Tony Seidita used when he mixed the meat.

At the deli one can also purchase a mini focaccia from a bakery in Chicago, pizza by the slice, spedini, and Roman Potato Salad, just to mention a few of the popular items on the menu. Then a table in the cafe beckons, and it's time for an Italian meal that didn't have to be cooked at home.

Shahrazad

2847 North Oakland
964-5476
Shorewood
Lunch and dinner every day
Non - smoking area
Bar - yes
MC, V, AE
Dress: fashionable

– middle eastern –

Many restaurant menus offer "generous toppings of feta cheese," or "hearty homemade soup," or even simply "homemade," and after eating, one questions the integrity of the promise. That will never happen at this Middle Eastern restaurant on Oakland Avenue. The portions are always generous, hearty means just that, and homemade lentil soup didn't start with a commercial base.

Shahrazad has a pleasant ambience, a bright airy space enhanced by Middle Eastern wall hangings. Everything on the menu is delicious, and if you can't pronounce the name of an entrée, or need help deciding what's for dinner, the waitstaff are helpful, patiently answering questions and making recommendations. The menu descriptions are excellent, for example "kibbee - a puree of seasoned bulgur layered with sautéed ground meat, onions and pine nuts, then baked and served with tabbouleh salad." That answers most questions, unless one wonders about "ground meat." Is it beef, chicken, pork or lamb? Ask your server.

Shorewood Inn

4473 North Oakland Avenue
964-2350
Shorewood
Lunch and dinner every day
Smoking - yes
Full bar
MC, V
Dress: wear your best Nancy North Shore Talbot's outfit

- plain good food -

The menu says the restaurant was established in 1995, but many of us have been going to the Shorewood Inn since the early 1970s. What happened in 1995 was the re-establishment of the Inn by Bill and Carol Meinhardt, along with son Jeff and daughter Barb. Thus the old-fashioned family touch is back, updated with fresh tulips on the tables and a bouquet of flowers in the women's room.

Shorewood Inn is a stuccoed-wall and German-timbered kind of place, where a veggie melt would never have been allowed on the menu twenty-five years ago. But in the 90s veggie is in, and the reviewers loved the $4.95 combination of mushrooms, red onion, green pepper, tomato and sprouts on whole wheat bread, covered with cheddar cheese and baked until it all melted together. This tasty economical meal is served with fries and coleslaw. If one stays away from the more expensive dinner entrees, that $10 bill will pay for a hearty meal. Burgers are $5 - $6 and a fantastic chef's salad costs $7.25. Looks like the new/old Shorewood Inn will be around in the next millennium.

Silver Spring House

6655 North Green Bay Avenue
352-3920
Glendale
Lunch and dinner every day
Smoking - in the bar only
Full bar
MC, V, AE
Dress: like the thirty-something generation

– bar food –

I've been a patron of the Silver Spring House since the early 70s, have probably sampled everything on the menu at least once, and can unconditionally recommend everything I've tasted. The food is fresh, portions generous, prices reasonable and even the service is impressive. Depending on when you come, the noise level varies from moderately quiet to desperately loud, especially on weekend nights starting at about 5:00 p.m. Contrary to what one would expect in a bar, the salads are outstanding; my favorite, the New Age Spinach Salad, is more than a meal.

The Silver Spring House was given Milwaukee County Landmark status in 1985. On this site in 1856, Charles Krocker built a log cabin tavern, the Krocker House. In 1902, one of his heirs sold his five acres and the fire-damaged cabin to John Kleist. Two years later, Kleist built a tavern north of the Krocker House, naming it the Silver Spring House. This tavern is the back dining room of the present Silver Spring House. Today's main dining room was a dance hall located behind the original tavern. In 1915, it was rolled on logs to the present location on Green Bay Avenue. In the 30s, the Friday fish fry cost 15 cents and the chicken fry 35 cents. In 1976 the current owners took over the tavern and the rest, as they say, is history.

Slim McGinn's

338 South 1st Street
271-SLIM
Walker's Point
Lunch and dinner every day
Smoking - yes
Full bar
MC, V, AE
Dress: early Goodwill and Doc Martens would go here

Bar food

There's no shortage of choices at Slim's, and I hear tell it's all good solid bar food with big portions and exceptional Saturday specials. Everyone loves the 12-ounce pork chop, and the boneless chop on a bun is good too, especially when treated with a teriyaki marinade. Slim's half-pound burgers are legend, char-grilled with cheese or however else you want to adorn the naked beef. On Sunday the Blue Plate Meatloaf, Lasagna, and Tenderloin Tips are each a full meal for $3.75.

Slim's has great old Milwaukee bar flavor with cream city brick walls and wooden plank tables. Something about Slim's menu looks a lot like McGinn's on Bluemound. Perhaps they're related?

Soda Fountain

1309 Milwaukee Avenue
571-1299
South Milwaukee
Breakfast and lunch, Tuesday - Sunday
Smoking - yes
Bar - no
Bring cash
Dress: a poodle skirt with saddle oxfords

– old fashioned diner food –

There's an Egg McMuffin and then there's the real thing, a breakfast sandwich at the Soda Fountain. The cook fries an egg, adds cheese and bacon, ham, or sausage, crams it inside a hard roll with more butter, and charges just $2.75 for this 1950s pre-cholesterol-conscious feast.

This is a tiny storefront restaurant, decorated 1950s-like, with aqua colored walls, a jukebox, and red and silver vinyl booths. Appliances and artifacts from that era are displayed. Tiny means two booths, one table, and eight stools. The walls are covered with fascinating signs and advertisements from the past.

Owner Lisa Bernier does the cooking, and that's by choice. She wanted to open a small place she could manage herself, with customers she knows by name, and a chance to do what she loves best, cook.

It's hard to spend much money here. Remember the fried egg sandwich from the 1950s? It's on the menu for $1.25, but cheese costs a quarter extra. At the high end, a five ounce tenderloin with eggs, potatoes and toast will set you back $6.50.

Sofia's

7032 West Lincoln Avenue
321-8600
West Allis
Lunch and dinner Tuesday - Sunday
Smoking - yes
Full bar
MC, V
Dress: flannel shirt and jeans

– somewhat italian –

This is your typical Milwaukee neighborhood restaurant starring good food, generous portions, moderate prices and a relaxed friendly atmosphere. Even the drinks are oversized and underpriced, as in the $2 - $3 range. Reviewers found the Shrimp Casino, prepared in a light tomato sauce and served over linguini, a delicious entree. Likewise, Eggplant Parmesan, rated excellent, cost only $6.95 and came with soup and garlic bread. The minestrone soup received unanimous "ayes," as did the "not too garlicky" garlic bread. Overall, Sofia's comes across as a good place to hang out with a group, and to enjoy an unrushed low budget meal in the company of other low-key diners.

The restaurant offers daily lunch and dinner specials, and to keep you coming back, tosses in a free cup of soup.

Solly's Coffee Shop

4629 North Port Washington Road
332-8808
Just west of Whitefish Bay
Breakfast, lunch, dinner Tuesday - Saturday
Smoking - no
No booze
MC, V
Dress: whatever feels good when you sit on a stool

- diner food -

Watch the waitresses at Solly's. They don't write orders, they memorize them. That's just one aspect of this high-quality, low-budget lunch counter that sets it apart from purveyors of franchise burgers. Lunch at Solly's means an EZ off and on the freeway, but don't look for a sign announcing their location close to the East Hampton exit from I 43. In 1970, they were displaced by that highway, and moved to their present location on the Port Road.

For 57 years this tiny lunch counter restaurant has served consistently good food. That's the reason people line up outside, and no one minds. Inside, twenty-four stools seat customers around two U-shaped counters. Friendly waitresses keep pace with a steady flow of burgers, fries, onions, and malts. Their motto hangs on the wall: "Food should be cooked with lots of love and lots of butter." They use plenty of both.

They're best known for burgers cooked in butter and served in a toasted bun with more melting butter oozing into the top of the meat. Malts here are so rich and thick they serve them right in the metal mixer. Solly's replicates a diner from the 40s, and sets an atmosphere of unhurried meals served by competent waitresses. Reviewers comments: "Definitely we will go back. We have already recommended it to friends. It may just be the hamburger-lover's alternative to fast food."

Soup Bros.

Around the corner from 2nd Street on Florida
860-SOUP
Walker's Point
6:00 a.m. - 6:00 p.m. Monday - Friday
11:00 a.m. - 4:00 p.m. Saturday
Smoking - no
Bar - no
Bring cash
Dress: your choice

– fabulous soup, also sandwiches and cookies –

I knew I'd found Soup Bros. when I drove south on 2nd
and spotted a dozen late model cars parked on Florida. Sure
enough, there was a sign and a doorway with a line of lunchtime
patrons spilling out onto the sidewalk. I found Richard Regner in
his tiny shop serving soup and sandwiches to go. When I visited in
April 1999, he had two tables for customers who chose to eat in,
but planned to expand the dining area and add a deck. Meanwhile
he'll dish up some of the best soup I've ever tasted. Because
Richard trained at the Culinary Institute of America (known
affectionately by insiders as the CIA), he has an admirable sense of
taste and quality, and all of his daily soups are truly superb. To
hear the daily menu, call 860-SOUP and listen to Chef Richard list
his selections.

Soup Bros. isn't just about soup. Richard starts his day at
6:00 a.m. baking bread for sandwiches. Tuna Salad with Capers,
and Country Ham with Cajun Jam are recommended, as are the
Chocolate Chunk cookies - not chips, chunks.

The idea for Soup Bros. came to Richard when he lived in New
York City, and noticed the lines that formed every day in front of
the legendary "Soup Nazi." His business, housed in a former
Schlitz Brewery Boarding House, may be Milwaukee's premier
purveyor of fine soup to go.

Speed Queen Bar-B-Q

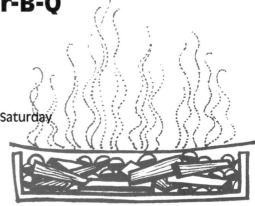

1130 West Walnut Street
265-2900
Downtown
Smoking - no
Lunch and dinner Monday - Saturday
Closed Sunday
No booze
Bring cash
Dress: anything washable

– carry-out –

You can eat in here, but most carry out. It's the place to come for barbecue extraordinaire!!! This is not to be confused with fast food. They smoke the beef, pork and chicken over a mix of hickory, oak, maple, and sweet applewood with a few charcoal briquettes tossed in; then they slice it thin and serve in a spicy full-flavored barbecue sauce. You can order your meat in a bun and call it a sandwich, or pile it on a plate and call it a meal. Dinner includes a choice of coleslaw, baked beans, and potato salad, and all of the above are also available a la carte. They also sell fried chicken, catfish, and perch, and unlike the Colonel's place, everything is cooked to order.

The beef-bar-b-q sandwich, a favorite, consists of a pile of sliced, smoked and sauced beef, crammed into a roll, served with crisp coleslaw, the perfect counterpoint to the spicy sauce. Don't try to be a neatnik - just order extra napkins.

Taco Amigo

4350 South 27th Street
282-7707
South Side
Lunch and dinner every day
Smoking - no
Full bar
MC, V, no checks
Dress: wear a serape and match the tablecloths

– mexican –

All the good Mexican cantinas aren't clustered around 5th and National, for here's gourmet Mexican chow in an unlikely location. Taco Amigo shares a building with Milwaukee Car Phones, across South 27th from Midas Muffler. Don't plan a U-turn going south if you miss it on the first drive-by, or you might end up on I-894. The "Authentic Mexican" sign above the brightly-lit Car Phone advertisement stands out, when they remember to turn it on.

The owner came to America in the early 1980s from Honduras, and for 12 years managed El Rey Products on South 5th. The menu diverges from tacos and tostadas into lesser known regional foods such as Nopalito Salad, Pozole, Mole Poblano, and two cactus specialties, Nopalito con Queso, and Nopalito with Chicken, Shrimp, and Beef. Whoever wrote the menu copy knew how to set a person's mouth to watering. "Pozole, the earthy character and flavor of the rich broth, corn and meat, with the crunchiness of raw vegetables and the spiciness of the sauce combine to give an incomparable sensation of flavors and textures."

On the down side, the reviewer noted the Sizzling Fajitas didn't sizzle, and while the menu promised a plate of assorted garnishes, the kitchen neglected to deliver them. They did better with the Nopalito garnish, remembering the lettuce but forgetting the tomato and guacamole. Gourmet? Ole!

Taqueria Azteca

2301 South Howell
486-9447
South Side
Breakfast, lunch and dinner Monday-Saturday
Smoking – no
Mexican beer (on Saturday the bartender will make special
  fruit margaritas)
Bring cash
Dress: sombrero optional

– mexican –

A visit to Taqueria Azteca is like a quick trip to Mexico. Spanish calendars, holy pictures, colored tin decoration on the walls, colorful tissue cut-outs strung across the ceiling, all are similar to the decor one would find in Mexican restaurants, especially around the time of All Saint's Day and Easter. They serve Mexican soda and Aguae Fresca Horchata, rice water and fruit drinks that taste just right with the sometimes spicy food.

If you find Mole Verde Estilo Oaxaca on the menu, don't hesitate to order this traditional stew. It's a mix of pork, cornmeal dumplings and white beans flavored with fennel and cilantro. At $8, it's a bargain.

Taquerias in Mexico are the equivalent of rapidly disappearing American sandwich shops. When one travels in Mexico, there's often a fine line between a taqueria and street food. They're inexpensive, might I say cheap by our standards, and they serve delicious, absolutely fresh foods prepared while one waits and perhaps sips a Negro Modolo.

I f traditional Mexican food served in an unpretentious space is your quest…

– here are four more –

Taqueria La Esmerelda
1108 W Greenfield
389-9789

Taqueria Los Comales
1306 South 16th
384-6101

Taqueria Chico's
1814 East North
Avenue
276-1277

Taqueria Jalisco
1035 South 16th
672-7070

Taste of India

10900 West Blue Mound Road
259-9200
Brookfield
Lunch Tuesday - Sunday
Dinner every day
Smoking - no
Full bar
MC, V, AE
Dress: business attire at noon

– indian –

To get the most food for your dollar, come to the lunch buffet. For $5.95 it's a bargain; they put out a variety of dishes, unlimited servings, and what's on the table will cost double at dinnertime. Taste of India won't win awards for décor, but who cares when one can feast on half a dozen Indian specialties and come back for seconds?

For the uninitiated, entrees are prepared mild, medium or hot, and hot means *hot*. The Chicken Saag, boneless chicken cooked with spinach is a classic dish. "Saag" refers to the addition of spinach in a curry. It cooks down to make a delicious creamy sauce.

There are five Biryani rice dishes on the menu. Biryani is an Indian rice casserole that's often garnished with nuts or dried fruit. They use basmati rice, Asian rice with a subtle nutty flavor.

The Tandoori Mixed Grill comes out of a tandoori oven, an oven made of clay designed to burn charcoal. Food cooked in it will have a flavor reminiscent of the process. The mixed grill includes two kinds of chicken, and seasoned beef baked on skewers and garnished with sautéed onions.

Ted's Ice Cream and Restaurant

6204 West North Avenue
258-5610
Wauwatosa
Breakfast, lunch Tuesday - Sunday
Friday open until 8:00 p.m. for their fish fry
Smoking - no
No booze
Bring cash, checks ok
Dress: comfy

– american –

It's written on a sign over the door: "Since 1941, the finest people on earth pass through this door...my customers." At 2:00 p.m. on an ordinary weekday, a few late lunch customers linger at the counter while strains of Louis Armstrong play softly in the background. Everyone appears to know everyone else.

Ted Gottwein opened his diner in 1941. In the 1950s son Ken took over, and since his death in 1991, his wife and daughter Patti have run the restaurant. Only the friendly faces change. The food, the low prices, and the homemade ice cream continue the 57-year tradition. It's a small place - just two U-shaped counters and four tables. They make ice cream on the premises, and the chocolate-chocolate chip-chunky peanut butter will satisfy discriminating ice cream aficionados. The only foods on the menu that aren't homemade are pastries from Meurer's Bakery.

Don't count on eating soup if you show up late for lunch. They make it daily, it's good, and occasionally gone by 2:00. The cheapest meals on the menu are grilled cheese or fried egg sandwiches (shades of the Depression) for $1.50. Even if you try, you can't spend much money here. $6.25 buys a beer batter Friday fish fry (pike) and for $3.50, they'll do an old fashioned belt-buster banana split where the whipped cream doesn't come from an aerosol can.

Thai Chef Restaurant

6735 West Lincoln Avenue
543-3381
West Allis
Lunch and dinner Monday - Saturday
Smoking - yes
Bar - no (only wine and Oriental plum wine)
MC, V
Dress: silk

– thai –

The small size of Thai Chef and its attractive table settings give it an intimate feeling, despite the fact that it's quite simple and unadorned. The seven tables are covered with white linen cloths and hunter green woven mats, and linen napkins are fanned inside tall glasses. Mirrored walls visually expand the interior.

The food is well prepared and servings generous. Reviewers found the entrees enormous after enjoying both appetizers and soup. Especially impressive was the Coconut Shrimp, lightly fried and served with a sweet and sour sauce. The Coconut Chicken Soup was also memorable, light and delicate with plentiful tender chunks of chicken breast hiding in the broth.

The evening special was Rama Chicken, tender chicken served in a peanut sauce surrounded by fresh crisp vegetables, and served with a large crock of streamed jasmine rice. Also recommended is a dessert, the Thai Chef Highlight Banana.

Thai Kitchen

2851 North Oakland Avenue
962-8851
Lower East Side
Lunch and dinner Monday - Saturday
Smoking - no
Bar - yes drinks available
Bring cash
Dress: silk

– thai –

The owners of this closet-size Thai restaurant have discovered the magic formula for a successful Lower East Side eatery. First, it's small. They're not paying for unused space, and unless the blizzard of '76 strikes again, they'll be busy every night. It's cozy, and if you want to know what to order, look around at your neighbors' entrees. If something looks good, ask.

That's how I found Volcano Chicken. It was irresistibly presented on a sizzling platter at an adjacent table. You won't find this dish in Thailand, but all the local Thai restaurants seem to feature it, and it makes a tasty and filling meal. It resembles fajitas, but the chicken is battered like a tempura, served on a bed of richly flavored grilled vegetables. This is a generous meal, and because it's so rich, one to share with a friend.

Patrons choose from "timid, hot, adventurous, or native Thai" seasoning, and we found "adventurous" to be warm, but certainly not hot. Vegetable Curry, mixed veggies in curry paste and coconut milk is a star. The coconut milk adds a silky creaminess to the dish as well as a healthy dose of fat. Could that be why it was so good?

Three Brothers Bar and Restaurant

2414 South St. Clair
481-7530
Bayview
Dinner Tuesday - Saturday
Smoking - yes
Full bar
Bring cash or a check
Dress: to linger

– serbian –

Three Brothers is located in a building constructed in 1897 for Schlitz Brewing Company, and today its Cream City brick exterior has been restored. This is Milwaukee's quintessential Old World restaurant, where they serve delicious food amid a charming mismatched mix of Formica tables, funky wooden chairs and oddball place settings. It has to be good, because owner Branko Radiecevich served Julia Child in 1990. Her press agent wanted Julia to "see not only the city's fancy spots but good home-cooking restaurants as well."

Branko uses only traditional family recipes from his native Yugoslavia and his Hungarian Goulash, Moussaka, and Stuffed Veal Breast are even better than they sound. Don't miss the Burek, a Serbian pastry made with phyllo dough layered with meat, spinach, or cheese and lots of butter. This golden brown three inch high flaky delight is what I dream about when I've been backpacking in the woods too long.

Because they bake everything to order, the pace might seem too leisurely. Come when you're not in a hurry. The house dinner salad is ordinary, but the Serbian salad with onions, tomatoes, feta, and oil and vinegar dressing is something else.

Tio Beta

565 West Lincoln Avenue
647-1430
South Side
Lunch and dinner Monday - Friday
Breakfast, lunch and dinner Saturday and Sunday
Smoking - no
Bar - yes
AE, checks ok
Dress: serape optional

– mexican –

When friends and I came to dinner at Tio Beta, we noticed a poster for Zacatecas, a city in north-central Mexico, on the wall. I have a fondness for the Zacatecas City Band, after I watched them perform while fireworks drifted onto their heads at a celebration in San Miguel de Allende. They never missed a beat, so when I learned the owner of Tio Beta came to Milwaukee from Zacatecas, I knew I would like my dinner.

There's a misconception about Mexican food, the assumption that it's always hot enough to cause heartburn, or acid indigestion. This theory can be proved absolutely wrong at Tio Beta if you order the Chili Relleno, or Camarones Rancheros, or Flautas. In each case the food is gently seasoned with the option of adding heat with the pico de gallo on the table.

The star of our meal was Camarones Ranchero, ten succulent shrimp in a red sauce. The sauce didn't overwhelm the delicate flavor of the shrimp, but added a nice edge to the dish. It held a hint of garlic and cinnamon.

You don't have to go to Mexico to get a perfect flan. Order one at Tio Beta, and you'll be licking your lips and wanting more.

TNT Mexican Restaurant

2797 South Kinnickinnic
483-6300
Bayview
Breakfast, lunch and dinner every day
Smoking - yes
Bar - good selection of Mexican beers
MC, V, AE
Dress: comfy

– mexican –

There are remnants here of former owner Gramma Emma, who moved to Las Vegas, for the space is huge and the upper level remains non-smoking. That's a good thing, because there are smokers seated close by, but the air up the single step is clear. With serapes hanging in the window and the Stones coming from the jukebox, the mood is upbeat. Bring a flashlight to find the restrooms; maybe the light was out the day I came for breakfast. My friend said he just made a lucky guess.

Our breakfast was impressive, and when I asked for pico de gallo instead of salsa, the chef made a dish for me on the spot. I smothered my Mexican Omelet, the special of the day, made with chorizo, a Mexican sausage, and nopales, cactus that's peeled and steamed, and the dish was all that I could ask for. My breakfast companion said his pancakes were good too. The bill for the two of us, including tax and tip, came to $10.

TNT has an extensive menu, but I would certainly recommend staying with the Mexican specialties such as beef, pork, chicken, and seafood dishes. Enough of the menu is in Spanish to tell you that they have an ethnic following in addition to gringos who love Mexican food. Someday I'll be brave and try the Menudo, or tripe soup, for breakfast.

Tommy's Rustic Inn

9909 West Appleton Avenue
463-5555
West Side
Lunch and dinner every day
Brunch on Sunday after 10:00 a.m.
Smoking - yes
Full bar
MC, V
Dress: jeans

– bar food –

Tommy's advertises "Milwaukee's Famous Hamburger," but that designation is debatable according to reviewers. No one said it was too greasy, however; instead the burger was a bit dry. That's good for weight-watchers, who may or may not want to add a basket of fries to the meal. The fries come highly recommended, chunky, served with flavored sour cream. If you're in the neighborhood, here's a value meal, though it may or may not be worth a drive across town.

Tom Thumb

1800 East Howard
489-1023
South Side
Lunch and dinner Monday - Saturday
Smoking - no
Bar - no
Bring cash
Dress: anything to make Tom and Ray smile!!!

– sandwiches and soup –

C heerful! In a word, that's the Tom Thumb sandwich and carryout restaurant. Recommended sandwiches are the Roast Beef, meat thinly sliced, stacked on a bakery bun; the Tuna Banquet, a heap of "dolphin free" tuna; the Atomic Thumb, salami, pepper cheese, red onion, and hot peppers; and the homemade chili with all the fixings. Everything is fresh, the soups are served hot and if you're feeling blue, stop by. Tom and Ray promise you'll leave with a grin on your face.

The Tracks

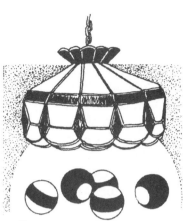

1020 East Locust Street
562-2020
Riverwest
Lunch and dinner (hours vary)
Smoking - yes
Full bar
MC, V, checks ok
Dress: jeans and tees

– pub food –

Here's good food in a bar setting. If you like a dim, smoky, sometimes crowded and noisy place, where the pub food rises way above average, then The Tracks is for you. Warning: it can get very busy at lunchtime.

They have the usual Tiffany lamps in the bar, a few tables, and a sports-dominated big screen video. In the back room there's a pool table, more dining tables, a few booths, and in the yard, a seasonal patio. You get plenty of food, i.e. your money's worth; the BLT might be the best in Milwaukee. Our reviewers will definitely return.

On Friday they serve Popcorn Shrimp, a generous mound of little ones along with fries, coleslaw, and a roll. Occasionally an overcooked tough shrimp finds its way into the basket, but then there are so many that one or two doesn't matter. It's not the same as eating five "jumbo" at a fancy place for a fancy price. The little shrimp are labor intensive, but worth the effort to peel each one separately. Other house specials include a boneless pork chop sandwich served with applesauce, and a chicken breast sandwich.

Turner Hall

1034 North Fourth Street
272-1844
Downtown
Lunch and dinner every day
Smoking - yes and no (they have a large non-smoking area)
Full bar
MC, V, checks ok
Dress: workout clothes optional, or lederhosen

– american/german –

In the early 1970's, the Turner Hall Friday fish fry was a steal at $1.65. Now they charge 1990s prices, but they still offer all-you-can-eat-plates of cod and perch plus cole slaw, potatoes, homemade tartar sauce and salty rye bread. In fact, the restaurant's fish fry was voted #1 by *Milwaukee Magazine* in 1998. For aficionados of potato pancakes, 95 cents buys a side order; that's two of the tastiest potato pancakes one will find in Milwaukee.

Turner Hall is run by the same corporation that owns Oakland Trattoria, Water Street Brewery, and Riverhouse Restaurant across from the Marcus Center for the Performing Arts. Each of these restaurants serves excellent food at reasonable prices. Turner Hall still offers a few German dishes as in the past, but the bulk of their menu tends toward more inexpensive and lighter meals, soups, and sandwiches. On the German menu, Chicken Schnitzel with Spaetzle is a house favorite. The spaetzle is sautéed in clarified butter, and it's euphoric.

The restaurant has been renovated and resembles a Schlitz Palm Garden, complete with lanterns and wall murals. The Turner organization dates back to 1809 and the University of Berlin. Their gymnastics program is well respected and their motto, "Sound Mind in a Sound Body," permeates all their non-eating activities.

Watts Tea Room

761 North Jefferson Street
291-5120
Downtown
Breakfast Monday - Friday
Lunch Monday - Saturday
High tea Monday - Saturday
Smoking - no
Bar - no
MC, V, AE
Dress: silk and lace

– elegant simple food –

The Watts Tea Room is a favorite downtown destination for people who appreciate gracious living. It's no secret there's a restaurant on the second floor of George Watts and Son Inc., a lovely shop that features crystal, silver, and objects of art, but one must know it's there to look for it. It's an elegant, large tearoom with damask draped windows looking out over Jefferson Street. The pressed flower and fern place mats give each diner a personal flower arrangement to admire. Food is served on Royal Worchester china, available for sale downstairs.

The food is always delicious. Each sandwich is made to order on whole wheat bread, unless one wishes a croissant, an additional $1. Our reviewers' favorite sandwich: mixed olive-nut, green and black olives, pecans, and a dressing, served on whole wheat bread with pickles on the side. A favorite dessert, the house special, Filled Sunshine Cake, a three layer sponge cake with French custard filling and seven-minute frosting. It's light and delicious, and not too sweet.

West Bank Cafe

732 East Burleigh
562-5555
Riverwest
Dinner every day
Smoking - no
Full bar
MC, V, AE
Dress: nicely

– vietnamese –

West Bank Cafe opened in the early 1970s in a renovated Riverwest storefront, as a delightful vegetarian restaurant. When the original owners moved on, the new owners Thanvanh Thi Ho and Diep Long Nguyen brought their Vietnamese cuisine to this well-established eatery. They first came to Milwaukee in 1975 and opened a small restaurant they called The Rose. When word spread, they found needed more space, so they moved to Capitol Drive, and in 1987 they moved again, this time to Burleigh. Wherever they went, their customers just kept coming. West Bank Cafe is a charming restaurant enhanced by a changing art exhibit, many plants, fresh flowers, and cloth table coverings.

The food is superb, and presented with careful attention to complex visual appeal, flavors, and textures. A hollow pineapple becomes a bowl overflowing with scallops and chicken in a mild orange sauce. The bread is warm and crusty; traditional Spring Rolls are studded with bits of shrimp, pork, and vegetables; the salad is filled with complementary colors and flavors.

What's Fresh

146 East Juneau Avenue
273-5677
Downtown
Breakfast, lunch and dinner weekdays
Saturday lunch
Smoking - no
Bar - no
Will take checks
Dress: downtown upscale

– sandwiches etc. (both carry-out and eat-in) –

If the question is "What's fresh?" the answer has to be, "Everything." Reasonable prices, abundant choices, and cheerful ambience make this small cafe a popular stop for downtowners. Sandwich prices vary from $2.35 for a half braunschweiger on rye with lettuce, tomato, onions, and sprouts, to $4.25 for a whole chicken-pecan sandwich. One can also order soup, salad, ice cream, chips, and cookies, plus juice, soda, and Milwaukee's own Sprecher Root Beer. La Boulangerie makes the bread and bakery for What's Fresh, and the soups and salads are made in-house.

I had to ask "What is an Angelo?" It's a hard roll or a bagel with two pieces of meat and two pieces of cheese served at breakfast.

For atmosphere, the owners hung dozens of lunch buckets from the ceiling, and the effect is similar to an upside down 1950s school cafeteria.

The Wild Thyme Cafe

231 East Buffalo Street
276-3144
Third Ward
Monday - Friday 11:00 a.m. - 2:00 p.m.
Smoking - no
No bar
MC, V, AE
Dress: business stylish (everyone else is)

– market fresh salads and sandwiches –

Around the corner from Broadway, on Buffalo, slightly off the main drag in the Third Ward is a gem, hiding behind a shop that will fascinate diners almost as much as the food at Wild Thyme. Looks like they're here to stay with this creative combo shop-dinette, where the early American look prevails, but business casual is the dress of the hour. And take note, they're only open for three hours, just enough time for a power lunch for downtown escapees.

The food has always been good, and continues to surprise first-timers. Everything is fresh with an accent on salads made with wild greens. Fresh Garden Salad is a meal, an abundant serving of vegetables on baby greens with homemade dressing. Choose from berry vinaigrette, honey mustard, ranch, or peppercorn parmesan. It's not easy to choose, so come again and then again, in order to sample all four.

If you're really hungry, order the Pasta and Sautéed Vegetables with or without grilled chicken breast. The serving is generous, enough for two meals, and the flavors spectacular. Polish this off with a mini dessert, selected from a tray filled with delectables, each $.50. A fine way to satisfy one's sweet tooth craving, and I speak for myself, without leaving with the stuffed feeling that often comes from eating "the whole thing."

William Ho's

3524 North Oakland Avenue
963-9781
Shorewood
Lunch and dinner every day
Smoking-yes
Full bar
MC, V
Dress: casual

– chinese –

An extensive menu and moderate prices bring regulars back for William Ho's Cantonese, Hunan and Indonesian specialties. Chicken Almond Ding with brown rice is a popular dish, perhaps because they serve generous portions of almonds and chicken plus many crisp crunchy sugar snap peas. The menu lists bounteous options for vegetarians, including a delicious entree they call Buddha Delight, a combination of carrots, bean sprouts, water chestnuts, baby corn, pea pods, tomatoes, celery, broccoli, bamboo shoots, and dried tofu reconstituted in flavored liquids.

Hard working UWM students without wheels appreciate William Ho's fast delivery service, and people with wheels appreciate the carryout option and the amazing number of choices on the menu. They advertise, "We have a full Chinese menu - you name it, we have it."

About the time this book went to the printer, William Ho's reinvented itself as a seafood restaurant. However, they kept the above-mentioned meals on the menu.

Zaffiro's

1724 North Prospect Avenue
289-8776
Lower East Side
Lunch and dinner Monday - Friday
Dinner Saturday and Sunday
Smoking - yes
Full bar
MC, V
Dress: casual

– italian, primarily pizza –

I remember when Dean Martin crooned "when the moon hits your eye like a bigga pizza pie, that's amore." In Indiana in the 50s, we thought Dean was saying "a big piece of pie," until we were introduced to the real thing at a bar, where Italians spun a yeast crust, covered it with tomato sauce and cheese, and called it "pizza." America's passion for pizza started in the 50s and you know the rest of the story. Today franchise pizza joints are as common as Wonder Bread, and businessmen, not Italians, run most of them. But Zaffiros is the real thing. Bobby and Rose Zaffiro opened their pizza restaurant/bar on Farwell in 1956, and with the exception of spreading into the adjacent barbershop, things have stayed the same for 43 years. Bobby Zaffiro is gone, but sons Mike and Joe took over in 1989 and kept the family business intact.

There isn't a better pizza in Milwaukee. One could call the sauce "antique," for it originated with Rose Zaffiro's mother in the 1930s, and remains unaltered and delicious. They also serve spaghetti, ravioli, and mostaccioli with or without a meat sauce. Try Zaffiro's Salad, and plan to share it with at least three friends. Everything's good here, soups, sandwiches, even the house Chianti Classico is reasonably priced and a good value. This is my favorite place to take out of town friends who want to see a classic neighborhood Milwaukee bar.

Zayna's

714 East Brady Street
226-9999
Lower East Side
Dinner carryout every day
No bar
No smoking
Bring cash
Dress: come naked if you wish, but wear a coat

– mostly pizza –

Zayna's is strictly carryout, a storefront on the west end of Brady Street. They used to occupy a tiny shop on North Avenue west of Humboldt, thus the move to the gentrified Brady neighborhood was a big one for Zayna's. Their main business is pizza, and that's what's recommended, especially the Supreme, topped with cheese plus onions, mushrooms, pepperoni, and sausage. They'll deliver at no cost if you live nearby, otherwise there's a nominal fee. In addition to pizza they'll fix chicken, seafood, Texas BBQ ribs, lasagna, a sub sandwich, a burger, or a gyros. Give Zayna's a try and welcome them to Brady Street.

Z's Cafe

7833 West Burleigh
445-1141
West Side
Breakfast, lunch and dinner Monday - Saturday
Smoking - yes
Bar - no
Bring cash
Dress: bring earplugs

– cafe food –

This is a small café, and that means the noise level will peak as crowd size increases. A popular breakfast hangout for locals, Z's, with its green plants in the window, diner decor and cheap prices, draws many families. There's counter service for twelve, the waitresses cruise the cafe to refill coffee cups, and if you're in a rush, count on prompt service. If your server is gossiping with a local, don't hesitate to interrupt. Breakfast Hash Brown Potatoes are crispy and were clearly homemade, the Greek Omelet filled with spinach and feta cheese is definitely recommended, and for calorie counters, they offer low-cal selections on the lunch and dinner menus. Any place where one can get two eggs, bacon, potatoes, toast, and coffee for $5.53 deserves a page in this book.

Late Entries - Not Reviewed, but Recommended.

Buck Bradley's
1019 Old World Third Street
224-8500
Charming 1890's saloon - try the steak

Coquette Cafe
316 North Milwaukee Street
291-2655
Sandy D'Amato's new place

El Babalu
611 West National
383-4044
In Walker's Point - unusual Mexican and Caribbean cuisine

Filippo's
6915 West Lincoln
321-4040
Family Italian restaurant

Filter Cafe, Inn
435 South 2nd
223-4613
In Walker's Point - appetizers, pasta, deli sandwiches and Soup Brothers soup

The Grecian Inn

14375 West Capitol
781-6333
No ordinary Greek family restaurant, they brought their Greek
dishes from North Avenue to Mayfair Road to the present
location

Joey's

1601 North Jackson
271-8401
Italian food - a Lower East Side landmark, across the street
from Dentrice Brothers

Mini's

6343 North Green Bay Avenue
247-9000
Has a great Friday fish fry complete with home made potato
pancakes; owner is a son of the family that owns Maniaci Cafe
Siciliano

New Hong Kong Buffet

1427 South 108th
258-8862
The name speaks for the menu

Thai Palace

838 North Old World Third Street
224-7076
Good buffet value at lunch

3 Hermones
1332 West Lincoln Avenue
384-9050
1100 West National
384-8850
Known for their seafood

Vinifera at the Passegio
1716 North Arlington Place
224-7076
Trendy new Brady Street restaurant, very well received

Z-Teca
3101 North Oakland Avenue
332-3000
2831 South 108th
321-3650
As advertised: "gourmet burritos" - an oxymoron?